Diane England

Cute Crochet
FOR
Kids

Martingale®
& COMPANY

Cute Crochet for Kids
© 2006 by Diane England

Martingale®
& COMPANY

Martingale & Company
20205 144th Avenue NE
Woodinville, WA 98072-8478 USA
www.martingale-pub.com

Printed in China
11 10 09 08 07 06   8 7 6 5 4 3 2 1

Credits

President ● Nancy J. Martin
CEO ● Daniel J. Martin
COO ● Tom Wierzbicki
Publisher ● Jane Hamada
Editorial Director ● Mary V. Green
Managing Editor ● Tina Cook
Technical Editor ● Donna Druchunas
Copy Editor ● Ellen Balstad
Design Director ● Stan Green
Illustrator ● Laurel Strand
Cover and Text Designer ● Regina Girard
Photographer ● Brent Kane

Mission Statement

Dedicated to providing quality products and service to inspire creativity.

Library of Congress Cataloging-in-Publication Data
Library of Congress Control Number: 2006014360

ISBN-13: 978-1-56477-707-2
ISBN-10: 1-56477-707-3

Contents

Introduction

Welcome to *Cute Crochet for Kids*. This book is written with a warm and affectionate smile and a tongue-in-cheek sense of humor. You'll discover that I love to make people laugh. I believe that there needs to be more love and laughter in the world.

"How did you come up with that design?" That is the question I am asked most often when people see me working on a project. I started making sweaters for my niece, Dallas. She is a skinny little flit of a thing who is always cold but does not like to wear store-bought sweaters. I made her a crocheted sweater from a pattern I found in a book. She loved it at first because it was, in her words, "pretty, not ugly." After a while, however, she stopped wearing it and I discovered a truth: children have trouble dressing themselves in clothing with the lacy structures for which crochet is so famous. My niece is very independent. If she can't dress herself, then she won't wear it, and the sweater I made for her was too difficult to put on.

I challenged myself. Could I design crocheted sweaters that children would want to wear? Could I design crocheted sweaters that weren't lacy and too difficult for immature reflexes to negotiate? Could I make children and adults laugh with pleasure? The designs in this book are the answer to that challenge. I hope this book sparks your creativity. Many of the patterns include design variations and suggestions for creating your own personal design.

This book was written to attract both new crocheters who have just entered the world of crocheting sweaters and advanced crocheters looking for a new challenge. The current interest in crochet has produced some great beginner crochet books. However, if you're more experienced, you might want to expand your crochet skills and learn new techniques, and the sweaters in this book are designed to help you do just that. They're also fun, colorful, and inventive.

On the following pages, you'll find 12 sweater designs ranging from beginner to experienced skill levels. The *beginner* project, Updated Renaissance Serf Tunic on page 57, is designed to give the crocheter who has been concentrating on making afghans the assistance to start crocheting sweaters. The pattern is both fun and great looking. If you have sewn your own clothes, you'll pick up sweater-making very easily because the same techniques apply, except that you use a crochet hook and yarn instead of a sewing machine and thread.

The three sweaters with an *easy* skill-level designation use basic stitches and easy shaping. They are perfect for the beginning crocheter trying to increase her skill level, as well as for anyone wanting to make something amusing. The ABCs Jazzy Pullover on page 6 features a new stitch called back single crochet (bsc) stitch. I cannot find a reference to such a stitch in any books, magazines, or on the Internet. It isn't the reverse single crochet (rsc) stitch with which we are all familiar. The back single crochet stitch is a single crochet stitch but the hook enters from the back of the piece rather than from the front of the piece. The puff pattern used in many of the sweaters uses this new stitch that is enjoyable to master.

The five sweaters designated as *intermediate* were designed to be entertaining with great texture and color, as well as to increase the crocheter's skill level by using more shaping, new techniques, and new stitches. The Birdhouse Cardigan on page 48 uses front-stitch double crochet (FSdc) and back-stitch double crochet (BSdc).

NOTE: These stitches are not front-post double crochet (FPdc) and back-post double crochet (BPdc) stitches. FSdc and BSdc don't raise the former row as much as FPdc and BPdc stitches do. FSdc and BSdc make a crocheted fabric that is less bulky and still has great texture, which is a more suitable fabric for a lightweight cardigan.

The three sweaters designated as *experienced* are my gifts to all the advanced crocheters out there waiting for a challenge, something new, and something to test their skills. I remembered you.

In the back of the book, you will find information that explores the important concepts of drape and gauge in crocheted sweaters and offers help for knitters who wish to successfully venture into the world of crocheting sweaters. You'll also learn about the tools you need, caring for your sweaters, stitch how-tos, and an abbreviation key.

The following section introduces some of the members of a knit and crochet group I meet with once a week. I include a list of quirky quips and quotes from the group that I have been recording for the last three years. Enjoy!

The Knitting and Crochet Club

I belong to the Knitting and Crochet Club of Rochester, New York, a small group of women who are all somewhere between the ages of 20 and 75. We meet in the coffee shop at a local bookstore on Monday nights. There's nothing like coffee, tea, gossip, and crocheting to set you up for the week. When we get together, our everyday lives recede to the corners of our existence. For a while, we stop being wives, mothers, aunts, and businesspeople and become crocheters and knitters—but mostly friends. I'd like you to meet my friends:

Ruby is the knitting "machinist" due to the unbelievable evenness of her stitch tension. She is a psychologist and the group's personal shrink.

Rollie is our queen bee—the one we turn to for advice with the fit, joining, or yarn-deficit problems we run into.

Lila is the group's ultimate lady. She knits and crochets. She makes the most beautiful scarves, shawls, and jewelry.

Pat is the group's dreamer. The knitting challenges she brings to the group have stretched and expanded our skills.

Zenia is the group's true switch hitter—she combines crochet and knitting to make some of the most wonderful items you'll ever see.

Joyce is the group's sage and "Florida Snowbird." She seams together the relationships of the group as easily as a knitted project.

Whether you are a new or seasoned crocheter, please consider joining a knitting and crochet group. I have never regretted any of the time I have spent with my group. (I cannot say the same for the time I have spent doing chores or working.) If there is no group in your area, start your own group. It's a great way to make new friends, as well as to learn new crochet skills as you work on the projects in this book.

Quips and Quotes from the Knitting and Crochet Club

A hole? That's not a hole! It's an air-conditioning duct.
After all, you don't want the sweater to be too hot!

The scarf is a little crooked but it's OK; my neck will never know it.

I meant to do that! I really think it adds something. Don't you?

That's how you know it's handmade. And as we all know,
handmade is *priceless* while machine-made is *boring*.

I multitask all the time. I can listen or talk while crocheting;
sometimes I do all three at once!

Buttons? Those aren't buttons! Those are my dreams.
I keep my dreams in jars. That way, I know where they are.

In the old days, Attention Deficit Disorder (ADD) was used rather than treated.
You just picked up some yarn and started making things.

Don't worry! We won't call the crochet police.

ABCs Jazzy Pullover

ABC

This jazzy little number will have your loved one singing a happy tune every time he or she slips into it. The blackboard features the basics of learning, and is a pocket to keep hands warm and treasures safe. This pullover has an oversized fit, making it perfect as a light coat for spring or fall. The tight weave of this stitch pattern will keep the wind from stealing the warmth from little bodies. For added protection from the elements, consider waterproofing the sweater to keep your little one warm and dry during soggy fall days and spring showers. There are several waterproofing sprays on the market—just be sure to reapply it after each wash. This pullover features a straight body, full sleeves, and a hood for added warmth on windy days. For an older child, replace the letters A, B, and C; the numbers 1, 2, and 3; and the crayons with a computer, world globe, or buttons of his or her favorite things.

Skill Level:

Easy ◼◼◻◻

Size:
24 mos (2, 4, 6X, 10, 12, 14)

Child's Chest Size:
20 (22, 24, 26, 28, 30, 32)"

Finished Chest Size:
24½ (26¾, 29, 31½, 34, 36¼, 37¾)"

Finished Sleeve Length:
8 (8½, 10½, 12, 13½, 15, 16)"

Finished Body Length:
12⅜ (13⅛, 14¾, 16, 17⅓, 18⅝, 20¼)"

Materials

3 (4, 4, 5, 5, 6, 7) skeins of Red Heart Kids from Coats & Clark (100% acrylic; 4 oz/113 g; 242 yds/221 m) in color 2930 Crayon 🄸

1 skein of Bernat Satin from Bernat (100% acrylic; 3.5 oz/100 g; 163 yds/149 m) in color 04040 Ebony 🄸

K-10.5 (6.5 mm) crochet hook or size required to obtain gauge for sweater

H-8 (5.0 mm) crochet hook or size required to obtain gauge for blackboard

Assortment of decorative buttons for pocket, such as letters, numbers, crayons, apples, school books, and pencils

Safety pins

Yarn pins

Gauge

Body: 13.2 sts and 16 rows = 4" in puff patt with size K-10.5 hook and Crayon yarn

Pocket: 15 sts and 17 rows = 4" in puff patt with size H-8 hook and Ebony yarn

Crochet Stitches

Applied slip stitch crochet, page 70

Back single crochet (bsc), page 70; this is *not* reverse single crochet

Single crochet (sc), page 70

Slip stitch (sl st), page 69

Puff Pattern

Row 1 (RS): Sc in first st and in each st across row, ch 1, turn.

Row 2 (WS): Bsc in first st and in each st across, ch 1, turn.

Rep rows 1 and 2 for patt.

Back

- With K-10.5 hook and Crayon yarn, ch 41 (45, 49, 53, 57, 61, 63). Sc in 2nd ch from hook and in each ch across—40 (44, 48, 52, 56, 60, 62) sts. Mark this side as RS with safety pin. Ch 1, turn.
- **Beg puff patt (WS):** Beg with row 2 of patt, work puff patt until piece measures 5¾ (6⅓, 6⅞, 7⅜, 8⅝, 9⅛, 10⅓)". Mark this row at both ends for armhole with safety pins.
- **Armholes:** Cont in puff patt until armholes measure 6⅞ (6⅞, 8, 8⅝, 9⅛, 9¾, 10⅓)". Tie off. Mark center st of neck with safety pin.

Front

- Work as for back until armholes measure 4⅝ (4⅝, 5⅛, 5¾, 6⅓, 6⅞, 7⅜)".
- **Shape neck:** Cont in puff patt, WORKING BOTH SIDES AT SAME TIME. Work first 16 (18, 20, 22, 23, 25, 26) sts.

Sk next 8 (8, 8, 8, 10, 10, 10) sts. With second ball of yarn, work rem 16 (18, 20, 22, 23, 25, 26) sts.

- Cont in puff patt, dec 1 st at neck edge every row 5 times—11 (13, 15, 17, 18, 20, 21) sts rem.
- Work even until armhole measures 6⅞ (6⅞, 8, 8⅝, 9⅛, 9¾, 10⅓)". Mark center st of neck with safety pin. Tie off.

Hood

- With size K-10.5 hook and Crayon yarn, ch 74 (78, 80, 81, 82, 84, 86). Sc in 2nd ch from hook and in each ch across—73 (77, 79, 80, 81, 83, 85) sts. Mark this side as RS with safety pin. Ch 1, turn.
- **Beg front band (WS):** Beg with row 2 of patt, work 5 (5, 5, 5, 5, 5, 7) rows of puff patt. Fold work in half so that row just finished lies next to first row. Make sc through 1 st in first row and 1 in last row tog. Cont working sc to join the 2 rows tog to end of row.
- **Work hood:** Beg with row 2 of puff patt, work 3 (5, 5, 3, 3, 5, 4) more rows. Dec 1 st at each end of next row, then every 3 (2, 2, 3, 3, 2, 2) rows 7 (8, 9, 8, 8, 9, 10) times—57 (59, 59, 62, 63, 63, 63) sts rem. Work even until piece measures 7⅓ (7⅜, 7⅝, 7⅞, 7⅞, 8⅛, 8⅛)", including front band. Tie off.

Sleeves (Make 2)

- With size K-10.5 hook and Crayon yarn, ch 25 (27, 28, 29, 31, 32, 33). Sc in 2nd ch from hook and in each ch across—24 (26, 27, 28, 30, 31, 32) sts. Mark this side as RS with safety pin. Ch 1, turn.
- **Beg puff patt (WS):** Beg with row 2 of patt, work puff patt, inc 1 st at each end of every 2 (2, 3, 3, 3, 3, 3) rows 1 (2, 9, 9, 11, 9, 15) time; then inc 1 st at each end of every 3 (3, 4, 4, 4,

4, 4) rows 8 (8, 2, 3, 3, 6, 2) times—42 (46, 49, 52, 58, 61, 66) sts.

• Work even until piece measures 8 (8½, 10½, 12, 13½, 15, 16)". Tie off.

Pocket

• Using size H-8 hook and Ebony yarn, ch 23 (27, 30, 31, 33, 36, 38). Sc in 2nd ch from hook and in each ch across—22 (26, 29, 30, 32, 35, 37) sts. Mark this side as RS with a safety pin. Ch 1, turn.

• Beg with row 2 of patt, work puff patt until piece measures 6 (6, 6, 6¼, 6¼, 6½, 6¾)". End after completing a WS row.

• Ch 1, sc in each sc around pocket placing 3 sc in each corner st, around to end, sl st to ch-1. Tie off.

• With WS facing you, reattach yarn to bottom-right corner of pocket. Holding hook on WS and yarn on RS of pocket, sl st in each st of foundation ch along bottom edge of pocket. Tie off.

• Matching center st of sweater front to center st of pocket, position pocket 3¼" from bottom of body. Attach pocket to body with yarn pins. Place safety pins 5 rows down from top of pocket and 9 rows up from bottom of pocket on each side of the pocket. Sew pocket to body, leaving space between safety pins on each side of pocket open.

TIP: For longer wearing, stitch across the edge at the bottom of the pocket and again one stitch up from the bottom. Repeat for the top.

• Arrange buttons and sew onto pocket.

Finishing

• **Side seams:** With pieces next to each other and WS up, weave side seams tog from bottom edge to armhole with sl st. See "Weave Stitch Joining with a Slip Stitch" on page 74.

• **Shoulder and sleeve seams:** With RS tog, sl st fronts to back at shoulder seams. Tie off. With RS tog, sl st underarm seams and sl st sleeves into armholes, easing to fit. Tie off.

• **Hood:** With WS facing you, attach center sts of hood and back tog. Secure with safety pin. Attach ends of hood to each corner of front neck, being sure to include fold ends of hood into neck seam. With WS tog, weave st seam tog, easing fit.

• **Body, neck, hood, and sleeve trim:** With WS facing you and size K-10.5 hook, attach Crayon yarn to side seam of bottom of body. Work applied sl st in each st of foundation ch along bottom edge of sweater. Tie off. Rep on each sleeve cuff and on neck edge from hood and across front. Tie off.

• Weave in ends. Mist with water and lay flat to dry.

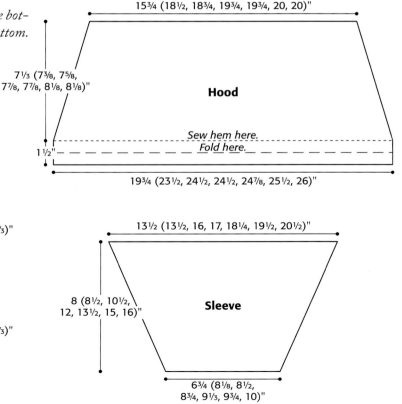

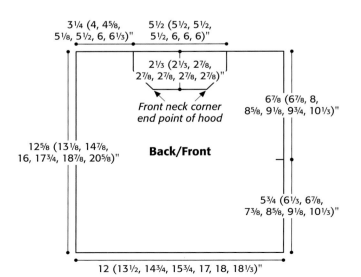

Blue Denim Cardigan with Scarf

This denim-looking sweater will be the talk of the school or church when your little one proudly wears it. It's also the perfect dog-walking coat for a dog-loving little lady. She will be in perfect style with this sweater, which features an attached scarf that can't be messed up, lost, or borrowed by her best friend. The buttons, which feature a dog wearing a green scarf, add the perfect finish to this design. You can use the same buttons or something similar. The sweater has an A-line body with a moderate fit, and cuffed, full-length, straight sleeves with a contrasting accent color. The sweater also features a subdued yet feminine hem at the bottom.

Skill Level:
Intermediate ◼◼◼◻

Size:
24 mos (2, 4, 6X, 10, 12, 14)

Child's Chest Size:
20 (22, 24, 26, 28, 30, 32)"

Finished Chest Size:
22¾ (24¾, 27, 29, 31, 33¼, 35¼)"

Finished Sleeve Length:
10½ (11, 13, 14½, 16, 17½, 18½)"

Finished Body Length:
12 (12½, 14¼, 15¾, 16½, 18, 19½)"

Materials

2 (2, 3, 3, 4, 4, 5) skeins of Wool-Ease from Lion Brand Yarn (80% acrylic, 20% wool; 3 oz/85 g; 197 yds/180 m) in color Denim Twist 194 (**4**)

1 skein of Red Heart Kids from Coats & Clark (100% acrylic; 5 oz/141 g; 302 yds/276 m) in color 2652 Lime (**4**)

I-9 (5.5 mm) crochet hook or size required to obtain gauge

5 (5, 5, 5, 6, 6, 6) dog buttons

Safety pins

Gauge

16 sc and 18 rows = 4" with size I-9 (5.5 mm) hook and Denim Twist yarn

Crochet Stitches

Single crochet (sc), page 70
Slip stitch (sl st), page 69

Body

- **Work as 1 piece (RS):** With Denim Twist yarn, ch 101 (109, 118, 133, 139, 145, 152) sts. Sc in 2nd ch from hook and in each ch across—100 (108, 117, 132, 138, 144, 151) sts. Mark this side as RS with safety pin. Ch 1, turn.
- **Beg sc:** Work in sc until piece measures ½" from beg.
- **Beg A-line shaping:** Cont in sc, dec 1 st at beg, 1 st in middle, and 1 st at end of next row. Dec 3 sts evenly along piece every 14 (14, 9, 11, 12, 12, 9) rows until 88 (96, 104, 112, 120, 128, 137) sts rem. Work even until piece measures 6¼ (6¼, 7½, 8½, 9, 9½, 10¾)".
- Split piece into 3 sections as follows:
- **Right front:** Working over first 22 (24, 26, 28, 30, 32, 34) sts only, cont sc until armhole measures 3 (3⅝, 3⅝, 4, 4½, 5, 5⅓)". End after working RS row.
- **Shape neck (WS):** Work over first 17 (19, 21, 23, 25, 27, 29) sts. Turn at neck edge, skipping last 5 sts for front neck. Beg with next row, dec 1 st at neck edge (right end) every row, until 13 (15, 16, 17, 20, 21, 23) sts rem.
- Work even until armhole measures 5⅓ (5¾, 6¼, 6¾, 7, 8, 8⅜)". Tie off.
- **Back (RS):** Work over next 44 (48, 52, 56, 60, 64, 69) sts. Work piece even until armhole measures 5⅓ (5¾, 6¼, 6¾, 7, 8, 8⅜)". Tie off.
- **Left front:** Cont working over last 22 (24, 26, 28, 30, 32, 34) sts. Work as for right front, beg neck shaping on RS row and working decs at left end of piece.
- **Shoulder seams:** With RS tog, sl st fronts to back at shoulder seams. Tie off.

Sleeves (Make 2)

Sleeves are joined to the shoulder and then worked in the round to the cuff. Each round is joined and then turned as if worked in rows.

- With RS facing you, attach Denim Twist yarn to bottom of armhole of bodice with sl st. Ch 1, sc in each st around armhole. Sl st to ch-1, turn. (The sl st counts as 1 st in each row.)

  NOTE: Count your stitches and record the number for crocheting the second sleeve.

- **Rnd 1 (WS):** Ch 1, sc in sl st of previous row and in each st around armhole, sl st to ch-1, turn.
- **Rnd 2 (RS):** Ch 1, sc in each st around to last st, sl st (over last st) to ch-1, turn.
- **Rnd 3:** Ch 1, sc in sl st of previous row and in each st around, sl st to ch-1, turn.
- **Rnd 4:** Ch 1, dec 1 st (using sl st and next st), sc in each st around to last 3 sts, dec 1 st, sl st to ch-1, turn.
- Rep rnds 1–4 until 30 (32, 34, 36, 38, 40, 42) sts rem, including sl st. Then rep rnds 1 and 2 until sleeve measures 10½ (12½, 14, 15, 15½, 17, 18)". Tie off.
- **Cuff trim:** With RS facing you, attach Lime yarn with sl st, ch 1, sc in each st around wrist, sl st to ch-1.
- **Next rnd:** Ch 1, sc in same st and in each sc around wrist, sl st to ch-1. Tie off.

Finishing

- **Buttonhole band:** *Right front* for girl. With RS facing you, attach Denim Twist yarn to bottom corner of cardigan with sl st, ch 1, sc in each st across front bodice, ch 1, turn.
- Sc in first st and in each st across, ch 1, turn.
- Mark positions for 4 (4, 4, 4, 5, 5, 5) buttons, placing first button ½" from bottom and last button ½" from top, and spacing rest evenly between these 2 positions.
- (Sc in each st to the position marked for the button, ch 3, sk next 3 sts, sc in next st); rep until all buttonholes are made, then sc in each rem st to end of band, ch 1, turn.

- (Sc in first st and in each st to buttonhole, place 3 sc around ch-3 sp); rep until all buttonholes are finished, sc in each st to end. Tie off.
- **Button band (RS):** *Left front* for girl sweater. Attach Denim Twist yarn to top corner of cardigan with sl st, ch 1, sc in each st of front, ch 1, turn.
- (Sc in first st and in each st across, ch 1, turn); rep 4 more times. Tie off.
- Sew buttons at marked positions on button band, being careful to align buttons with buttonholes.
- **Body trim:** With RS facing you, attach Denim Twist yarn to lower-left corner of bottom hem. Ch 1, sc in each st along bottom of sweater to other side, ch 1, turn.
- Sc (working over sts of previous row) in each st along sweater bottom, ch 1, turn.
- Sc (working over sts of 2 previous rows) in each st along sweater bottom. Tie off.

Scarf Collar

- With WS facing you, attach Lime yarn to top edge of button or buttonhole band with sl st, ch 1, sc in first st and in each st around neck, including sts of button and buttonhole bands, ch 1, turn.
- (Sc in first st and in each st around neck, ch 1, turn); rep 4 more times.
- (Sl st in first st, sc in 2nd st, sc in each st around neck, ch 1, turn. Sl st in first 2 sts, sc in rem sts around neck, ch 1, turn); rep 4 more times.

- Sl st in first 5 sts, sc in rem sts around neck, ch 1, turn.
- Sl st in first st, sc in second st, sc in each st around neck, ch 1, turn.
- Sl st in first 7 sts, sc in rem sts around neck, ch 1, turn.
- Sl st in first st, sc in second st, sc in each st around neck, ch 1, turn.
- Sl st in first 13 sts, sc in rem sts around neck, ch 1, turn.
- (Sk first st, sc in second st, sc in each st around neck, ch 1, turn); rep until 1 st remains at tip of scarf. Tie off.
- **Scarf trim:** With RS facing you, attach Lime yarn to corner of scarf at button band with sl st, ch 1, sc in each st around neck, ch 1, turn. Sl st in each st around scarf, being sure to place a (ch 1, sc, ch 1) at tip of scarf, cont around scarf with sc to beg. Tie off.
- With Lime yarn, *loosely* tack scarf to sweater at back, at top corners of scarf and at tip, making just enough sts to hold scarf in place but not so many that it looks sewn on. The idea is to make scarf appear as though it's moving.
- **Button loop:** Attach Lime yarn to bottom corner of scarf above buttonhole band with sl st, ch 8, sl st to top of scarf above buttonhole band. Tie off.
- Position button off center on scarf from rest of buttons, aligning it with button loop. Sew on button.
- Weave in ends. Mist with water and lay flat to dry. Fold up sleeve cuffs if desired.

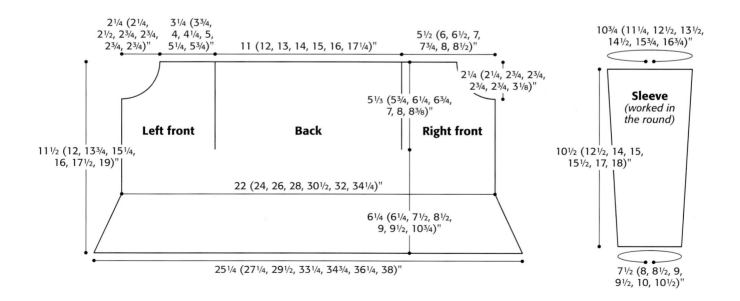

2¼ (2¼, 2½, 2¾, 2¾, 2¾, 2¾)"

3¼ (3¾, 4, 4¼, 5, 5¼, 5¾)"

11 (12, 13, 14, 15, 16, 17¼)"

5½ (6, 6½, 7, 7¾, 8, 8½)"

10¾ (11¼, 12½, 13½, 14½, 15¾, 16¾)"

2¼ (2¼, 2¾, 2¾, 2¾, 2¾, 3⅛)"

5⅓ (5¾, 6¼, 6¾, 7, 8, 8⅜)"

Left front   **Back**   **Right front**

Sleeve *(worked in the round)*

11½ (12, 13¾, 15¼, 16, 17½, 19)"

22 (24, 26, 28, 30½, 32, 34¼)"

10½ (12½, 14, 15, 15½, 17, 18)"

6¼ (6¼, 7½, 8½, 9, 9½, 10¾)"

25¼ (27¼, 29½, 33¼, 34¾, 36¼, 38)"

7½ (8, 8½, 9, 9½, 10, 10½)"

Teacher's Pet Cardigan

If you have a little one about to start or return to grade school, this regular-length, straight cardigan with a moderate fit will be perfect in the classroom and on the playground. The red yarn used for the "bricks" in this sweater can be changed to a different color depending on the wearer's preferences. This sweater is an experienced-level project due to the nap of the fabric created and the use of a two-yarn crochet technique.

Skill Level:
Experienced ◼◼◼◼

Size:
24 mos (2, 4, 6X, 10, 12, 14)

Child's Chest Size:
20 (22, 24, 26, 28, 30, 32)"

Finished Chest Size:
25½ (27½, 29, 30¼, 33, 35¾, 38¼)"

Finished Sleeve Length:
7¾ (8¼, 10¼, 11¾, 13¼, 14¾, 15¾)"

Finished Body Length:
13½ (14½, 16¼, 17½, 18¾, 20, 21)"

Materials

2 (2, 3, 3, 3, 4, 4) skeins of Encore Worsted from Plymouth Yarn Company (75% acrylic, 25% wool; 3½ oz/100 g; 200 yds) in color Red 9601 ④

2 (2, 2, 2, 2, 3, 3) skeins of Wool-Ease from Lion Brand Yarn (86% acrylic, 10% wool, 4% rayon; 3 oz/85 g; 197 yds/180 m) in color Wheat 402 ④

1 skein of Wool-Ease from Lion Brand Yarn (80% acrylic, 20% wool; 3 oz/85 g; 197 yds/180 m) in color Grey Heather 151 ④

J-10 (6.0 mm) crochet hook or size required to obtain gauge

K-10.5 (6.5 mm) crochet hook (optional for collar)

4 (4, 5, 5, 5, 5, 6) schoolhouse buttons

Safety pins

Gauge

13.2 sts and 6 rows of bricks = 4" in brick wall patt with size J-10 hook and Red and Wheat yarn

NOTE: Work rows 1 and 2 of the brick wall pattern to crochet one row of bricks.

Crochet Stitches

Back single crochet (bsc), page 70; this is *not* reverse single crochet

Double crochet (dc), page 71

Half double crochet (hdc), page 71

Single crochet (sc), page 70

Slip stitch (sl st), page 69

Brick Wall Pattern

The brick wall pattern is made with different-size bricks in each row to make a realistic-looking brick design. As you work the brick wall pattern, make the bricks a different size on each row. I've included instructions for making 5-, 6-, and 7-stitch bricks. You can make the bricks any size you like as long as you don't work fewer than 2 double crochets (Red) or more than 7 double crochets (Red) for each brick. Randomly change your pattern and just have fun.

Basic Brick Wall Pattern

Row 1 (RS): With Wheat yarn, ch 1, working over Red yarn, then sc in each st across occasionally catching Red yarn in sc to secure Red yarn. Keep Wheat yarn attached. Turn.

Row 2 (WS): With Wheat yarn, ch 3 (counts as first dc here and throughout). Working over Red yarn, make 1 dc with Wheat, *change to Red yarn, working over Wheat yarn, make 1 dc in each of next 5 sts, change to Wheat yarn, working over Red yarn, make 1 dc in next st*; rep from * to * to last st. Change to Wheat yarn, working over Red yarn, make last dc in Wheat. Turn.

NOTE: Always end row 2 by making one double crochet with Wheat, even if the last Red double crochet portion is smaller or larger than the pattern.

Rep rows 1 and 2 for patt.

5-Stitch Brick Wall Pattern (Shorthand)

Row 1 (RS): Ch 1 (Wheat), sc (Wheat) in each st across.

Row 2 (WS): Ch 3 (Wheat), *5 dc (Red) in next 5 sts, dc (Wheat) in next st*; rep from * to * to last st, dc (Wheat).

Rep rows 1 and 2 for patt.

6-Stitch Brick Wall Pattern (Shorthand)

Row 1 (RS): Ch 1 (Wheat), sc (Wheat) in first st and in each st across.

Row 2 (WS): Ch 3 (Wheat), *6 dc (Red) in next 6 sts, 1 dc (Wheat) in next st, 5 dc (Red) in next 5 sts, 1 dc (Wheat) in next st, 3 dc (Red) in next 3 sts, 1 dc (Wheat) in next st*; repeat from * to * to last st, dc (Wheat).

7-Stitch Brick Wall Pattern (Shorthand)

Row 1 (RS): Ch 1 (Wheat), sc (Wheat) in first st and in each st across.

Row 2 (WS): Ch 3 (Wheat), *7 dc (Red) in next 7 sts, 1 dc (Wheat) in next st, 4 dc (Red) in next 4 sts, 1 dc (Wheat) in next st, 3 dc (Red) in next 3 sts, 1 dc (Wheat) in next st*; repeat from * to * to last st, dc (Wheat).

Puff Pattern

Row 1 (RS): Sc in first st and in each st across row, ch 1, turn.

Row 2 (WS): Bsc in first st and in each st across, ch 1, turn.

Rep rows 1 and 2 for patt.

Body

- **Work as 1 piece:** With size J-10 hook and Grey Heather yarn, ch 82 (89, 94, 98, 107, 116, 124). Sc in 2nd ch from hook and in each ch across, ch 1, turn—81 (88, 93, 97, 106, 115, 123) sts. Mark this side as RS with safety pin. (Sc in each st across, ch 1, turn); rep once more.
- **Start brick wall patt (RS):** Change to Wheat yarn. Beg with row 1 of patt, work even in brick wall patt until piece measures 5¼ (6¾, 8, 8, 9⅓, 9⅓, 10¾)", excluding Grey Heather hem. End after completing row 1 (Wheat row), even if this means that piece is a bit longer than specified.
- Split piece into 3 sections as follows:
- **Left front (WS):** Beg with row 2, work brick wall patt over first 20 (22, 23, 24, 26, 29, 31) sts only. Work even until armhole measures 4 (4, 4, 5⅓, 5⅓, 5⅓, 5⅓)". End after working a WS row.
- **Shape neck (RS):** Work over first 15 (17, 18, 19, 21, 24, 26) sts. Turn at neck edge, skipping last 5 sts for front neck. Beg with next row, dec 1 st at neck edge

(left end) every row, until 11 (13, 14, 15, 17, 20, 22) sts rem.

- Work even until armhole measures 6¾ (6¾, 6¾, 8, 8, 9⅓, 9⅓)". End after working row 1 (Wheat row), even if this means that piece is a bit longer than specified. Tie off.
- **Back (WS):** Attach Red and Wheat yarn. Beg with row 2 of brick wall patt, work over next 41 (44, 47, 49, 54, 57, 61) sts only, being sure to match brick wall patt of left front. Work back of piece even until armhole measures total of 6¾ (6¾, 6¾, 8, 8, 9⅓, 9⅓)". End after working row 1 (Wheat row), even if this means that piece is slightly longer than specified. Tie off.
- **Right front (WS):** Attach Red and Wheat yarn. Starting with row 2 of brick wall patt, cont patt over rem 20 (22, 23, 24, 26, 29, 31) sts. Work as for left front, beg neck shaping on a WS row and working decreases at right end of piece. End after working row 1 (Wheat row), even if this means that piece is slightly longer than specified. Tie off.
- **Shoulder seams:** With RS tog and Wheat yarn, sl st fronts to back at shoulder seams. Tie off.

Sleeves (Make 2)

Sleeves are worked sideways. The center of sleeve is worked first, and then side shaping.

- With size J-10 hook and Wheat yarn, ch 28 (30, 34, 37, 41, 47, 51) sts.
- **Beg brick wall patt (RS):** Sc in second ch from hook, sc in each ch across, turn. Piece should measure approx 7 (7½, 9½, 11, 12½, 14, 15)" long after second row is complete.
- Attach Red yarn, cont with brick wall patt until sleeve measures 8 (8, 8, 11, 11, 12¼, 12¾)" wide. End after working sc (Wheat) row.
- **Beg sleeve shaping (WS):** Cont with row 2 of brick wall patt to last 6 sts of sleeve, then with Red, hdc in next st, sc in next st, sl st in next st. Switch to Wheat, ch 1, turn. Sl st into sc of last row, then sc in each st to end of sleeve, ch 3, turn.
- Measure sleeve and mark ½ and ¾ position of sleeve length (measured from wide end of sleeve, which is shoulder; see sleeve diagram on page 19). Cont with row 2 of brick wall patt to 3 sts before ¾ mark, with Red, hdc in next st, sc in next st, sl st in next st. Switch to Wheat yarn, ch 1, turn. Sl st into sc of last row, then sc in each st to end of sleeve, ch 3, turn.

- Cont with row 2 of brick wall patt to last 3 sts before ½ mark, with Red, hdc in next st, sc in next st, sl st in next st. Switch to Wheat yarn, ch 1, turn. Sl st into sc of last row, then sc in each st to end of sleeve, ch 3, turn. Tie off.
- With WS facing you, attach Red and Wheat yarn to 4th st from narrow wrist end of sleeve with sl st. With Red, sc in next st, hdc in next st, cont with row 2 of brick wall patt to end of row. With Wheat, ch 1, turn.
- Sc (Wheat) in each st to ¾ position, drop Red yarn at this position, cont to sc to 4th st from wrist, sl st in next st, ch 1, turn.
- Sk first st, sl st (Wheat) in next st and in each st to ¾ position of sleeve. Pick up Red yarn and with Red, sl st in next st, sc in next st, hdc in next st, cont with row 2 of brick wall patt to end of row, ch 1, turn.
- Sc (Wheat) in each st to ½ position, drop Red yarn at this position, cont with sc (Wheat) to sl st of previous row, sl st in next st, ch 1, turn.
- Sk first st, sl st (Wheat) in next st and in each st to ½ position of sleeve. Pick up Red yarn and with Red, sl st in next st, sc in next st, hdc in next st, cont with row 2 of brick wall patt to end of row, ch 1, turn.
- Sc (Wheat) in each st to sl st (Red), sl st in next st, ch 1, turn.

- Do not tie off. Cut Red yarn.
- **Sew sleeve seam:** With Wheat yarn and RS of sleeve tog, sl st seam along long edge of sleeve. Tie off.
- **Sew sleeve into armhole:** With RS tog, place seam of sleeve at bottom of armhole so that seam will be under arm. Adjust position of sleeve to match brick patt of sleeve to brick patt around armhole. Sl st to armhole with Wheat yarn, easing to fit. Tie off.
- **Cuff trim:** With RS facing you, attach Wheat yarn to wrist of sleeve with sl st, ch1, sc in each st around, sl st to ch-1. Tie off.
- With RS facing you, attach Grey Heather yarn to wrist of sleeve with sl st. Ch 1, sc in each st around wrist, sl st to ch-1. Ch 1, sc in each st around wrist, sl st to ch-1. Ch 1, sl st in each st around wrist. Tie off.

Collar

The instructions below involve making a small standup section that hugs the neck and a collar that folds over and spreads flat against the top of the sweater. If you would like a fuller collar, increase the number of stitches 10% to 20% when you change to the looser gauge. For a flatter collar, increase the number of stitches immediately after pickup.

- **Setup:** With RS facing you and using size J-10 hook, attach Grey Heather yarn to edge of neck of bodice with sl st. Ch 1, sc in first st and in each st to shoulder seam, place 2 sc in shoulder seam, then sc in each st to center of back neck, 2 sc in center st, sc in each st to opposite shoulder seam, 2 sc in shoulder seam, then sc in each st to opposite side of neck, ch 1, turn.
- **Row 1 (WS):** 1 bsc in first st and in each st around neck to opposite corner, ch 1, turn.
- **Row 2 (RS):** 2 sc in first st, 1 sc in each st to center st, 2 sc in center st, 1 sc in each st to opposite corner, 2 sc in corner.
- Rep row 1 once more.
- Loosen your gauge or switch to size K-10.5 hook to achieve a looser gauge. Work in looser gauge for remainder of collar. A looser gauge will allow collar to lie better. Rep row 2 once.
- Rep rows 1 and 2 until collar is 2 (2, 2, 2½, 2½, 2½, 3)" wide, excluding first 3 rows. Tie off.

Finishing

- **Buttonhole band:** *Right front* for girl, *left front* for boy. With RS facing you, attach Grey Heather yarn to bottom of front edge (girl) or top of front edge (boy) with sl st. Sc in each st along cardigan front, ch 1, turn.
- Sc in first st and in each st along cardigan front, ch 1, turn.
- Mark positions for 4 (4, 5, 5, 5, 5, 6) buttons, placing first one ½" from bottom of band and last one ½" from top of band, and spacing rest evenly between these two positions.
- (Sc in first st and in each st to position marked for button, ch 3, sk next 3 sts, sc in next st); rep until all buttonholes are made, then sc in each rem st to end of band, ch 1, turn.
- (Sc in first st and in each st to buttonhole, place 3 sc around the ch-3 sp); rep until all buttonholes are finished, sc in each st to end. Tie off.
- **Button band:** *Left front* for girl, *right front* for boy. With RS facing you, attach Grey Heather yarn to top of front edge (girl) or bottom of front edge (boy) with sl st. Sc in each st along cardigan front, ch 1, turn.
- (Sc in first st and in each st along cardigan front, ch 1, turn); rep 3 more times. Tie off.

- Sew buttons at marked positions on button band, being careful to align buttonholes with buttons.
- **Body trim:** With RS facing you, attach Grey Heather yarn with sl st to lower corner of sweater. Ch 1, sc in each st around perimeter of sweater, placing 3 sc in each corner st, sl st to ch-1.
- Ch 1, sl st in each st around perimeter of sweater, sl st to ch-1. Tie off.
- Weave in ends. Mist with water and lay flat to dry.

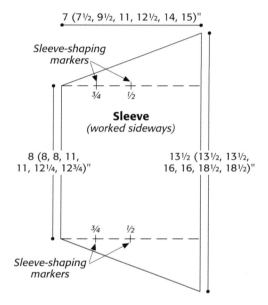

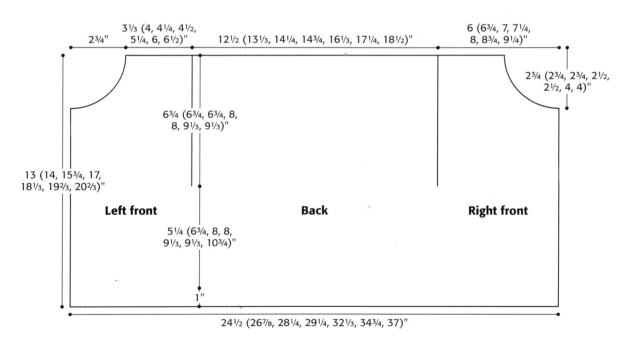

Ivy League Pullover

It's never too early to start inspiring the little academic in your family to reach the highest echelons of education. And this ivy-bedecked, boatnecked pullover, with its moderate fit and straight body, will keep your future college student comfortable and warm while she hits her books in style.

Skill Level:
Intermediate ◼◼◼◻

Size:
24 mos (2, 4, 6X, 10, 12, 14)

Child's Chest Size:
20 (22, 24, 26, 28, 30, 32)"

Finished Chest Size:
22¾ (25¼, 27, 30, 31¼, 33¼, 35¾)"

Finished Sleeve Length:
4 (4½, 6, 7, 8, 9⅓, 10)"

Finished Body Length:
12¼ (13, 14½, 16, 17⅓, 18½, 20⅓)"

Materials

2 (3, 3, 3, 4, 4, 5) skeins of Wool-Ease from Lion Brand Yarn (80% acrylic, 20% wool; 3 oz/85 g; 197 yds/180 m) in color Forest Green Heather 180 ▣

2 (2, 3, 3, 3, 4, 4) skeins of Wool-Ease from Lion Brand Yarn (80% acrylic, 20% wool; 3 oz/85 g; 197 yds/180 m) in color Grey Heather 151 ▣

J-10 (6.0 mm) crochet hook or size required to obtain gauge

2 pkgs of ivy leaf buttons

Safety pins

Gauge

Lower body: 13 sts and 12 rows = 4" in alternating rows of sc row and hdc with size J-10 (6.0 mm) hook

Upper body and sleeves: 7 sts and 9 rows = 4" in star st patt with size J-10 (6.0 mm) hook

Crochet Stitches

Beginning star stitch, page 72

Half double crochet (hdc), page 71

Ivy stitch (3-spike cluster), page 72

Overstitching, page 70

Single crochet (sc), page 70

Slip stitch (sl st), page 69

Star stitch, page 72

Back

- **Beg lower body:** With Forest Green Heather yarn, ch 38 (42, 45, 49, 52, 55, 59) sts, sc in second ch from hook and in each st across, ch 1, turn—37 (41, 44, 48, 51, 54, 58) sts.

- Sc in first st and in each st across, ch 1, turn.

- Working in back lps only, sc in first st and in each st across. Mark this side as RS with safety pin. Ch 1, turn.

- (Sc in first st and in each st across, ch 1, turn); rep 2 more times.

- **Work ivy st (RS):** Attach Grey Heather yarn and keep Forest Green Heather yarn attached. *With green yarn (working over grey yarn) work 4 sc, switch to grey yarn (working over green yarn), work ivy st*; rep from * to * until 5 or fewer sts rem, switch to green yarn (working over grey yarn) and work rem sts in sc. Ch 1, turn. Cut grey yarn.

- With green yarn, sc in first st and in each st across, ch 1, turn.

- Working in back lps only, sc in first st and in each st across, ch 1, turn.

- Sc in first st and in each st across, ch 2 (counts as 1 hdc), turn.

- (Hdc in second st and in each st across, ch 1, turn. Sc in first st and in each st across, ch 2, turn.); rep until piece measures 6¼ (6¼, 7, 8, 9, 9, 9¾)". End this section with a sc row, even if this requires adjustments in length to achieve. Tie off.

- **Beg sleeves and upper body (RS):** With grey yarn, ch 22 (24, 26, 28, 30, 30, 32) sts. Attach the ch formed to left edge of bodice with sl st. Tie off. Attach grey yarn to right edge of bodice with sl st, ch 23 (25, 27, 29, 31, 31, 33) sts. Sc in 2nd ch from hook, sc in each ch and st across to end of other grey ch, turn.
- **Star st row (RS):** Work beg star st, then change to star st and work across piece, ch 1, turn.
- **Sc row (WS):** Work 2 sc in eyelet of first star, sc in next st, *sc in next eyelet, sc in next st*; rep from * to * across.
- Cont alternating rows of star st and sc until armhole measures 6 (6¾, 7½, 8, 8⅓, 9¼, 10⅝)". Tie off.

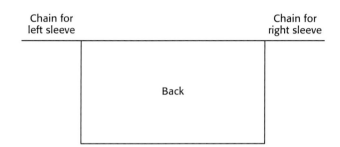

Chain for left sleeve

Chain for right sleeve

Back

Front

Work as for back.

Finishing

- Mark center st of both front and back.
- Leave center 7 (7¼, 7¾, 8, 8½, 9, 9¼)" of top of bodice open for neck.
- **Seams:** With RS tog, making sure that bottom trims match and correct space is left for neck, sl st shoulder, side, and sleeve seams.
- **Overstitching:** Using photo as guide, attach green yarn to top of bodice in grey area with sl st. (Ch 5, sl st to bodice); rep in this fashion, making wavy patt around top portion of pullover. Tie off.
- Sew buttons randomly on sweater, making sure stem of each leaf is touching vine.
- **Bottom trim:** With RS facing you, attach green yarn to bottom of body. Sl st in each edge st around bottom. Tie off.
- Weave in ends. Mist with water and lay flat to dry.

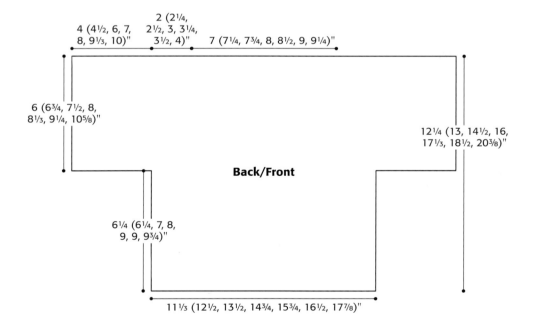

2 (2¼, 2½, 3, 3¼, 3½, 4)"

4 (4½, 6, 7, 8, 9⅓, 10)"

7 (7¼, 7¾, 8, 8½, 9, 9¼)"

6 (6¾, 7½, 8, 8⅓, 9¼, 10⅝)"

12¼ (13, 14½, 16, 17⅓, 18½, 20⅜)"

Back/Front

6¼ (6¼, 7, 8, 9, 9, 9¾)"

11⅓ (12½, 13½, 14¾, 15¾, 16½, 17⅞)"

Teddy Bear Chanel-Style Jacket

This little jacket is the fastest pattern imaginable. You'll be surprised at how quickly you'll finish this lovely little creation, which will make your loved one look like a warm, cuddly teddy bear. If the sweater is a gift, I suggest the addition of a teddy bear to complete the look.

This sweater has straight styling, a moderate fit, full-length sleeves, and a blue ribbon for a collar. Consider changing the ribbon color to your child's favorite color to personalize it, or you may wish to let the child choose the color.

Skill Level:
Intermediate ◼◼◼▭

Size:
2 (4, 6X, 10, 12, 14)

Child's Chest Size:
22 (24, 26, 28, 30, 32)"

Finished Chest Size:
25¾ (27¼, 30, 32, 34, 36¼)"

Finished Sleeve Length:
8½ (10½, 12, 13½, 15, 16)"

Finished Body Length:
15 (15⅓, 17¾, 20, 21, 22¾)"

Materials

2 (2, 3, 4, 4, 4) skeins of Wool-Ease Thick & Quick from Lion Brand Yarn (86% acrylic, 10% wool, 4% rayon; 6 oz/170 g; 108 yds/98 m) in Wood 404 ⑥

1 skein of Microspun from Lion Brand Yarn (100% microfiber acrylic; 2.5 oz/70 g; 168 yds/154 m) in color Lilac 144 ③

N-13 (9.0 mm) crochet hook or size required to obtain gauge for body

H-8 (5.0 mm) crochet hook or size required to obtain gauge for ribbon collar

2 teddy bear buttons

1 silver clasp

Safety pins

Yarn pins

Gauge

Body: 6.6 sts and 8.0 rows = 4" in puff patt with size N-13 (9.0 mm) hook and Wood yarn

Ribbon collar: 13 sts by 16 rows = 4" in puff patt with size H-8 (5.0 mm) hook and Lilac yarn

Crochet Stitches

Back single crochet (bsc), page 70; this is *not* reverse single crochet

Single crochet (sc), page 70

Slip stitch (sl st), page 69

Puff Pattern

Row 1 (RS): Sc in first st and in each st across row, ch 1, turn.

Row 2 (WS): Bsc in first st and in each st across, ch 1, turn.

Rep rows 1 and 2 for patt.

Body

• **Work as 1 piece:** With size N-13 hook and Wood yarn, ch 44 (46, 50, 54, 57, 61). Sc in 2nd ch from hook and in each ch across—43 (45, 49, 53, 56, 60) sts. Mark this side as RS with safety pin. Ch 1, turn.

• **Beg puff patt (WS):** Beg with row 2 of patt, work puff patt until piece measures 9 (9⅓, 10¾, 12, 13, 13¾)". End after working a WS row.

• Split piece into 3 sections as follows:

• **Right front (RS):** Work patt over first 11 (11, 12, 13, 14, 15) sts only, cont puff patt until armhole measures 3 (3, 4, 5, 5, 6)".

• **Shape neck (WS):** Work over first 8 (8, 9, 10, 11, 12) sts. Turn at neck edge, skipping last 3 sts for front neck. Beg on next row, dec 1 st at neck edge (right end) every row, until 6 (6, 7, 8, 9, 10) sts rem. Work piece even until armhole measures 6 (6, 7, 8, 8, 9)". Tie off.

• **Back (RS):** Work over next 21 (23, 25, 27, 28, 30) sts. Work even until armhole measures 6 (6, 7, 8, 8, 9)". Tie off.

• **Left front (RS):** Cont working over rem 11 (11, 12, 13, 14, 15) sts. Work as for right front, beg neck shaping on RS row and working decs at left end of piece. Tie off.

• **Shoulder seams:** With RS tog, sl st fronts to back at shoulder seams. Tie off.

Sleeves (Make 2)

Sleeves are joined to the shoulder and then worked in the round to the cuff. Each round is joined and then turned as if worked in rows.

- With RS facing you and size N-13 hook, attach Wood yarn to bottom of armhole with sl st. Ch 1, sc in first st and in each st around armhole, sl st to ch-1. Turn.

  NOTE: Count your stitches and record the number for crocheting the second sleeve. The slip stitch counts as one stitch in each row.

- **Rnd 1 (WS):** Ch 1, working in sl st of previous row, bsc in first st and in each st around to last st, sk last st, sl st to ch-1. Turn.

- **Rnd 2 (RS):** Ch 1, working in sl st of previous row, sc in first st and in each st around to last st, sk last st, sl st to ch-1. Turn.

- Rep rnds 1 and 2, dec 1 st every 5 rows until you have 16 (16, 18, 21, 20, 23) sts.

- Work even until sleeve measures 8½ (10½, 12, 13½, 15, 16)".

- Ch 1, sl st in each st around wrist, sl st to ch-1. Tie off.

Ribbon Collar

- With size H-8 hook and Lilac yarn, ch 91 (102, 111, 120, 128, 138). Sc in 2nd ch from hook, sc in each st across—90 (101, 110, 119, 127, 137) sts. Mark this as RS with safety pin. Ch 1, turn.

- (Sc in first st and in each st across, ch 1, turn); rep 4 more times.

- Work sc in each st around perimeter of ribbon, working 3 scs in each corner, sl st to first sc, ch 1, turn. Sl st in first st and in each st around perimeter, placing a (sl st, ch 1, sl st) in each corner. Tie off.

Finishing

- **Body trim:** With RS facing you, attach Wood yarn to bottom edge of body with size N-13 hook, sl st evenly around entire edge of bodice, placing a (sl st, ch 1, sl st) in each corner. Tie off.

- Sew clasp and buttons on to ribbon.

- Weave in ends. Mist with water and lay flat to dry.

- With WS tog, pin center st in back of sweater neck to center of ribbon along long side. Then fold ribbon over neck to outside so that it covers neck edge. Adjust ribbon so that it hangs evenly. Invisibly tack ribbon to neck edge with needle and Lilac yarn just under edge of ribbon collar.

- *Using photo as guide, draw one end of ribbon up to form loop at neck, and leave rest of end hanging. Twist loop at neck and tack it to jacket with Lilac yarn. Arrange ribbon so that it looks like it's moving, and place end of ribbon toward back of jacket to make it look as if it's being blown by wind. Tack ribbon to jacket with a few invisible sts.* Rep from * to * on other end of ribbon.

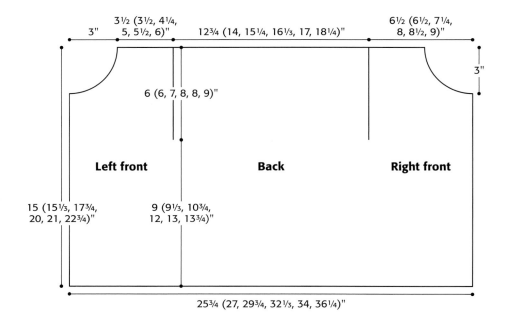
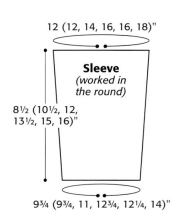

Pink Fantasy Sweater

This beautiful sweater is perfect for the little darling in your life. The delicate, lacy sweater has a comfortable fit, A-line shaping, full-length straight sleeves, and a round jewel neck. It features a magnificent, handmade glass button reminiscent of cameo brooches. You can find handmade buttons at your local yarn shop or craft store, or on the Internet. If you want to make your very own special button, your local craft store should have everything you need.

The yarn used for this sweater is 100% nylon and washes up wonderfully (my niece "tested" it out with cranberry juice). The number of steps in the crochet pattern requires that this design be assigned an experienced skill level. The use of a row counter for this sweater will save on frustration. I know that from experience!

Skill Level:
Experienced ◼◼◼▶

Size:
6 (12, 18, 24) mos

Child's Size:
10 lbs (18 lbs, 24 lbs, 20")

Finished Chest Size:
24 (26, 28, 27)"

Finished Sleeve Length:
6½ (7, 7½, 8½)"

Finished Body Length:
12 (12, 13½, 13½)"

Materials

2 (2, 3, 3) skeins of Velvet Touch by Wendy (100% nylon; 50 g; 105 m) in color Pink 1209 🄷
F-6 (4.0 mm) crochet hook or size required to obtain gauge
1 magnificent button

Gauge

16 sts and 11 rows = 4" in body patt with size F-6 hook

Crochet Stitches

Double crochet (dc), page 71
Half double crochet (hdc), page 71
Modified popcorn stitch (m-pc), page 73
Single crochet (sc), page 70
Slip stitch (sl st), page 69

Trim Band Pattern

Row 1 (WS): Sc in 2nd ch from hook and in each ch across, ch 3 (counts as dc), turn.

Row 2 (RS): Dc in 2nd st and in each st across, ch 1, turn.

Row 3: Sc in each st across, ch 1, turn.

Row 4: Working in back lps only, sc in first st, *hdc in next st, sc in next st*, rep from * to * to last st, hdc in last st, ch 1, turn.

Row 5: Sc in first hdc, *hdc in next sc, sc in next hdc*, rep from * to * to last st, hdc in last sc, ch 1, turn.

Rows 6–11: Rep row 5.

Row 12: Working in back lps only, sc in each st across, ch 3 (counts as 1 dc in body patt), turn.

Body Pattern

Row 1 (WS): Dc in second st and in each st across, ch 4 (counts as first dc and ch 1), turn.

Row 2: Dc in 2nd st (1 st added), *sk 1 st, ch 1, dc in next st, rep from * to * to end of row, ch 3 (counts as 1 dc), turn.

Row 3: Dc in first ch sp and in each st and ch sp across, ch 1, turn.

Row 4: Sc in second st (1 st removed) and in each of next 2 sts, *work m-pc around post of dc in previous row, sc in each of next 9 sts*, rep from * to * across to last 4 sts, work m-pc in next st, sc in last 3 sts, ch 1, turn.

Row 5: Sc in each st across, ch 4 (counts as first dc and ch 1), turn.

Row 6: Rep row 2.

Row 7: Dc in first ch sp and in each st and ch sp across, ch 3 (counts as dc), turn.

Row 8: Working in back lps only, sc in 2nd st (1 st removed) and in each st across, ch 3, turn.

Row 9: Dc in second st and in each st across, ch 4 (counts as first dc and ch 1), turn.

Work rows 1–9 once, then rep rows 2–9 for patt.

Body

- **Work as 1 piece:** Ch 101 (111, 119, 111) sts loosely. Use larger hook size if necessary.
- Work rows 1–12 of trim band patt.
- **Beg A-line shaping:** Beg body patt, dec 3 (3, 1, 3) sts evenly across first row of patt—97 (107, 117, 107) sts rem.
- Dec 1 st every 6 (8, 8, 12) rows until 92 (100, 108, 104) sts rem. Work even until piece measures 5¾ (5¾, 6½, 6½)".
- Split piece into 3 sections as follows:
- **Right front (RS):** Working over first 23 (25, 27, 26) sts only, cont body patt until armhole measures 2¼ (2¼, 3, 3)", work 4 rows of dc, work row 2 of body patt once, work 1 row of sc. AT SAME TIME, beg neck shaping when armhole measures 4⅜ (4⅜, 5⅛, 5⅛)".
- **Shape neck (WS):** Work over first 18 (20, 22, 21) sts. Turn at neck edge, skipping last 5 sts for front neck. Beg on next row, dec 1 st at neck edge (right end) every row until 15 (15, 17, 16) sts rem.
- Work even until armhole measures 5¾ (5¾, 6½, 6½)". Tie off.
- **Back (RS):** Work over next 46 (50, 54, 52) sts only. Work patts as for front without shaping until armhole measures 5¾ (5¾, 6½, 6½)". Tie off.
- **Left front:** Cont working over rem 23 (25, 27, 26) sts. Work as for right front, beg neck shaping on RS row and working decs at left end of piece.

- **Shoulder seams:** With RS tog, sl st fronts to back at shoulder seams. Tie off.
- **Buttonhole band (RS):** *Right front.* Attach yarn to bottom corner of cardigan with sl st, ch 1, sc in each st along edge of bodice, ch 1, turn.
- (Sc in each st along edge of bodice, ch 1, turn); rep once more.
- Sc in first 3 sts, ch 5 (or as many as necessary to make buttonhole), sk next 5 sts (to match buttonhole size), sc in each st of band, ch 1, turn.
- Sc in each st of band, placing 5 sc in 5-ch sp, ch 1, turn.
- Sc in each st along band. Tie off.
- **Button band:** *Left front.* With RS facing you, attach yarn to top corner of cardigan with sl st, ch 1, sc in each st up front edge of front, ch 1, turn.
- (Sc in each st across, ch 1, turn); rep 3 more times. Tie off.

Sleeves (Make 2)

Sleeves are joined to the shoulder and then worked in the round to the cuff.

- With RS facing you, attach yarn to bottom of armhole with sl st. Ch 1, sc in each st around armhole, sl st to ch-1.

NOTE: Count your stitches and record the number for crocheting the second sleeve.

- **Rnd 1:** Ch 1, sc in first st, 1 hdc in next st, *sc in next st, hdc in next st; rep from * around. Join to ch-1 with sl st.
- **Rnd 2:** Ch 3 (counts as dc in this row and foll rows), 1 dc in each st around. Join to ch-3 with sl st.
- **Rnd 3:** Ch 1, sc in first st, 1 hdc in next st, *sc in next st, hdc in next st; rep from * around. Join to ch-1 with sl st.
- **Rnd 4:** Ch 3, *ch 1, sk next st, dc in next st, rep from * around armhole, dec 1 st in this row. Join to ch-3 with sl st.
- Rep rnds 1–4 until sleeve measures 6 (6½, 7½, 8)".
- **Ruffle edging:** Ch 2, 2 hdc in same st, *sl st in next st, 3 hdc in next st, rep from * around wrist, join with sl st. Tie off.

Finishing

- **Body trim:** With RS facing you, attach yarn to corner of bottom hem. Ch 1, sc in each st around perimeter of sweater including neck edge, placing 2 sc in each corner st, ch 1, turn.
- **Ruffle edging:** Worked only along the bottom edge of the sweater, ch 2, 2 hdc in first 2 sts, *sl st in next st, 3 hdc in next st*; rep from * to * to last 3 sts, 1 hdc in each of last 3 sts. Tie off.
- Sew button at marked position on button band, being careful to align button with buttonhole.
- Weave in ends. Mist with water and lay flat to dry.

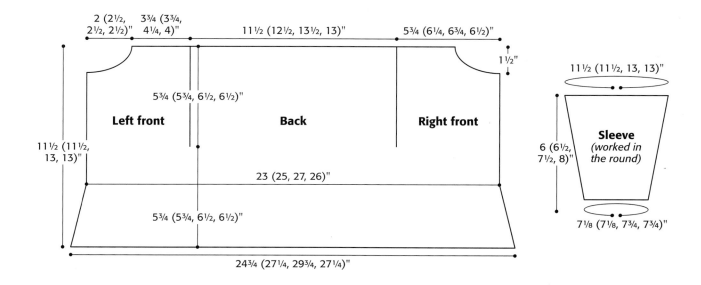

Cherry Pie Vest

Does the little girl in your life love cherry pie? Well, this beautiful vest will be just the thing to make her day. This vest features a comfortable fit, straight styling, a stand-up partial collar, and cherry buttons, completing the look to delicious perfection. If you'd like to add sleeves, refer to the optional sleeve directions at the end of the project. To see a picture of how the sleeves will look, refer to the photo on page 46 in Beehive Vest, which features the same sleeves. This sweater is at the experienced skill level. But don't be discouraged. If you love it, practice with some other patterns in this book, and then tackle this one.

Skill Level:
Experienced ◼◼◼▭

Size:
2 (4, 6X, 10, 12, 14)

Child's Chest Size:
22 (24, 26, 28, 30, 32)"

Finished Chest Size:
24¾ (27, 29½, 31½, 33, 35½)"

Finished (Optional) Sleeve Length:
8½ (10½, 12, 13½, 15, 16)"

Finished Body Length:
12 (13¾, 15½, 16½, 18½, 18¼)"

Materials for Vest

2 (2, 2, 2, 3, 4) skeins of Caron Simply Soft from Caron International (100% acrylic; 6 oz/170 g; 330 yds) in color Red 9729 (4)

1 (2, 2, 2, 2, 2) skeins of Caron Simply Soft from Caron International (100% acrylic; 6 oz/170 g; 330 yds) in color Off White 9702 (4)

H-8 (5.0 mm) crochet hook or size required to obtain gauge

5 (5, 5, 6, 6, 6) cherry buttons

Safety pins

Yarn pins

Yarn for Sleeves (Optional)

1 (2, 2, 3, 3, 3) skeins of Caron Simply Soft from Caron International (100% acrylic; 6 oz/170 g) in color Off White 9709 (4)

Gauge

Body: 14 sts and 9 rows = 4" in cherries patt with size H-8 (5.0 mm) hook

Piecrust lattice strips: 15 sts = 4" in piecrust lattice strip patt with size H-8 (5.0 mm) hook

Trim and sleeves: 9 sts and 12 rows = 4" in woven patt (do not count the ch-1 sps) with size H-8 (5.0 mm) hook

Crochet Stitches

6-cluster stitch (6-CL), page 73

7-cluster stitch (7-CL), page 73

Overstitching, page 70

Single crochet (sc), page 70

Slip stitch (sl st), page 69

Cherries Pattern

Row 1 (RS): Sc in first 2 sts, *7-CL in next st, sc in next 3 sts*; rep * to * to last 2 sts, sc in last 2 sts, ch 1, turn.

Row 2 (WS): Sc in first 4 sts, *7-CL in next st, push cherry to RS, sc in next 4 sts*; rep * to * to last 4 sts, sc in last 4 sts, ch 1, turn. Cherries in this row fall in between cherries in previous row.

Rep rows 1 and 2 for patt.

NOTE: Always end row 1 with 2 single crochets and row 2 with 4 single crochets even if you have to leave out a cluster.

Notes for a More Realistic Look

The pattern for the cherries is a regular repeat pattern. If you're comfortable experimenting, try randomizing the position of the cherries (clusters), as well as altering the size of the cherries by changing the number of loops on the hook from 7 to 4, 5, or 6 for each cluster.

Another way to enhance this pattern is to exchange some of the cluster stitches with puff stitches (page 73) or popcorn stitches (page 72).

Piecrust Lattice Strip Pattern

Row 1 (RS): Ch 4, *sl st into 2nd ch from hook (peak formed), ch 3, rep from * until piecrust lattice strip is length required, ch 3. Turn.

Rows 2–4: Sc in 2nd ch from hook and in each st across, ch 1, turn.

Row 5: Sc in first 3 sts, *ch 2, sl st into sc just made below chains, sc in next 2 sts, rep from *, sc in last 2 sts. Tie off.

Woven Pattern (Collar and Optional Sleeves)

This pattern must be worked on an even number of stitches.

Row 1: Ch 1, sc in first st, ch 1, *sk 1 st, sc in next st, ch 1*; rep from * to last st, sc in last st, turn.

Row 2: Ch 1, sc in first st, *ch 1, sk 1 st, sc in ch-1-sp*; rep from * to last st, sc in last st, turn.

Rep row 2 for patt.

Body

- **Work as 1 piece:** With Red yarn, ch 83 (91, 99, 106, 112, 120). Sc in 2nd ch from hook and in each ch across—82 (90, 98, 105, 111, 119) sts. Mark this side as RS with safety pin. Ch 1, turn.
- Sc in first st and in each st across, ch 1, turn.
- **Beg cherries patt (RS):** Beg with row 1 of cherries patt, work even until piece measures 5⅓ (6¼, 7, 8, 9, 9)". End after working WS row.
- Split piece into 3 sections as follows:
- **Right front (RS):** Work cherries patt over first 19 (21, 23, 25, 26, 28) sts only. Cont cherries patt until armhole measures 4½ (4½, 4½, 4½, 4½, 5⅓)".
- **Shape neck (WS):** Work cherries patt over first 13 (15, 17, 19, 19, 21) sts. Turn at neck edge, skipping last 6 (6, 6, 6, 7, 7) sts for front neck. Beg with next row, dec 1 st at neck edge (right end) every row, until 10 (12, 14, 15, 15, 17) sts rem.
- Work even until armhole measures 6¼ (7, 8, 8, 9, 9¾)". Ch 1, turn, sc in first st and in each st across, ch 1, turn. Sc in each st across. Tie off.
- **Back (RS):** Cont cherries patt over next 44 (48, 52, 55, 59, 63) sts only, being sure to match right front. Work back of piece even until armhole measures total of 6¼ (7, 8, 8, 9, 9¾)". Tie off.

- **Left front (RS):** Cont cherries patt over rem sts. Work as for right front, beg neck shaping on RS row and working decs on left end of piece.
- **Shoulder seams:** With RS tog, sl st fronts to back at shoulder seams. Tie off.

Piecrust Lattice Strips

The vertical strips extend from the bottom of the sweater on the front, up and over the shoulder, then down to the bottom of the sweater on the back. The ends of the strips are attached to the bottom hem. The horizontal strips extend around the sweater and are attached to the front edges. Shorter strips are used on the upper body between the armholes. Use the photo as a guide, or arrange the strips however you like them. The number of strips you want to put on your vest is up to you. It depends on what you think a cherry pie should look like.

- Measure length needed for strip (do this loosely for ease of fit). With Off White yarn, work row 1 of piecrust lattice strip patt until strip is correct length. Work rows 2–5 of piecrust lattice strip patt. Tie off.
- Make as many strips as desired and arrange on bodice, weaving strips just as you would piecrust on cherry pie. Attach piecrust strips to body with yarn pins or safety pins.
- When all strips are positioned correctly, tack strips to bodice with needle and Off White yarn.
- With RS facing you, attach Off White yarn to corner of vest, ch 1, sc in each st across, placing (sc, ch 1, sc) in each corner st around perimeter. Be careful to include edges of piecrust lattice strips in the turn. Tie off.

NOTE: Be sure to tack down both sides of the piecrust lattice strip to prevent curling. Do not tack down the peaks of the piecrust lattice strips. For a cleaner look, weave the needle into the red yarn to disguise the tacking, even from the inside of the garment.

High, Round Collar

- With RS facing you, attach Off White yarn to edge of front neck with sl st at position of 3rd CL row down from shoulder, ch 2, sc in same st, ch 1, [*sk next st, sc in next st, ch 1*; rep from * to * to shoulder seam, place (sc, ch 1, sc) in shoulder seam]; rep around neck to 3rd CL row down from shoulder on opposite side. Be sure that collar is positioned equally around neck.
- Work woven patt for 3 more rows. Tie off.

Finishing

- **Buttonhole band:** *Right front* for girl. With RS facing you, attach Off White yarn to bottom corner of vest front with sl st, ch 1, sc in each st across front. Ch 1, turn.
- Sc in first st and in each st across, ch 1, turn.
- Mark positions for 5 (5, 5, 6, 6, 6) buttons, placing first one ½" from bottom and last one ½" from top, and spacing rest evenly between these 2 positions.
- (Sc in first st and in each st to position marked for button, ch 2, sk next 2 sts, sc in next st); rep until all buttonholes are made, then sc in each rem st to end of band, ch 1, turn.
- (Sc in first st and in each st to buttonhole, place 2 sc around ch-2 sp); rep until all buttonholes are finished, sc in each st to end. Tie off.
- **Button band:** *Left front* for girl. With RS facing you, attach Off White yarn to top corner of vest front with sl st, ch 1, sc in each st of front, being careful to include edges of piecrust lattice strips in trim, ch 1, turn.
- (Sc in first st and in each st across, ch 1, turn); rep 2 more times. Tie off.
- Sew buttons at marked positions on button band, being careful to align buttons with buttonholes.
- **Trim:** Attach Off White yarn to lower-right corner of vest, ch 1, sc in first st and in each st evenly up front band, cont around perimeter of bodice placing (sc, ch 1, sc) in each corner st, sl st to ch-1. Ch 1, sc in first st and in each st around perimeter, placing 3 sc in each corner st.
- Sl st in each st around perimeter of vest, adding a ch 1 at each corner. Tie off.

Armholes

- **Armhole trim:** With WS facing you, attach Off White yarn at bottom of armhole and under lip of armhole with sl st ½" from edge (see figure on page 70).
- Using overstitching, ch 1, sc evenly around inside of armhole, sl st to ch-1. This will be connection for optional sleeve. Rep on 2nd armhole.
  NOTE: Only trim armholes after attaching the piecrust lattice strips. Be sure to include the piecrust lattice strip edges in this trim.

Optional Sleeves (Make 2)

Sleeves are joined to the armhole trim at the shoulder and then worked in the round to the cuff. Each round is joined and then turned as if worked in rows.

- With RS facing you and size H-8 hook, attach Off White yarn to armhole trim at underarm with sl st. Ch 1, sc evenly around armhole to underside of trim, sl st to ch-1.
  NOTE: Count your stitches and record the number for crocheting the second sleeve. Make sure you have an even number of stitches.
- Ch 1, beg woven patt, working in the round, remembering to join each rnd with sl st to ch-1 before turning. Dec 1 st at each end of every 4 rows, until 28 (28, 30, 32, 32, 34) sts rem.
- Work even until sleeve measures 8½ (10½, 12, 13½, 15, 16)". Tie off.
- Weave in ends. Mist with water and lay flat to dry.

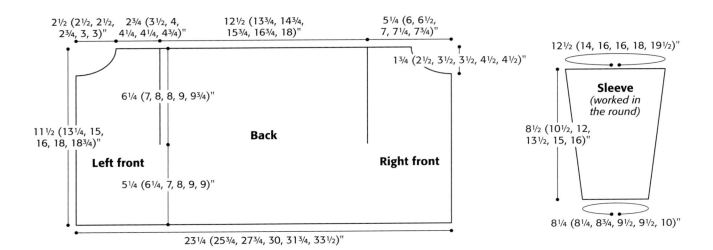

Picture Perfect Pullover

The family artist or art lover will love this little pullover. You can use the designs presented here for your pictures, copy a favorite painting you admire, or assemble a picture of your own. You could also invite the little one you're making the sweater for to choose the picture. It would be a wonderful joint project for the both of you to share and enjoy. Just be careful when using "flying" insect buttons. As you can see in the model, a butterfly has "escaped" from the picture and is flitting around the neck of the pullover. This two-tone pullover has cropped sleeves, drop shoulders, a straight body, and a keyhole front collar.

Skill Level:
Easy ◼◼☐☐

Size:
24 mos (2, 4, 6X, 10, 12, 14)

Child's Chest Size:
20 (22, 24, 26, 28, 30, 32)"

Finished Chest Size:
24½ (27¼, 28½, 31¼, 32½, 34, 36½)"

Finished Sleeve Length:
7 (7, 7, 7, 8⅓, 8⅓, 8⅓)"

Finished Body Length:
15 (17, 17, 18½, 20, 21½, 22¼)"
including tails

Yarn for Pullover

1 (1, 1, 2, 2, 2, 2) skein of Caron Simply Soft from Caron International (100% acrylic; 6 oz/170 g; 330 yds) in color Light Country Blue 9709 **4**

1 skein of Caron Simply Soft from Caron International (100% acrylic; 6 oz/170 g; 330 yds) in White 9701 **4**

Yarn for Picture Frame

2 skeins of Red Heart Luster Sheen from Coats & Clark (100% acrylic; 4 oz/113 g; 335 yds/306 m) in color 0604 Gold **3**

Yarn for Picture Canvases

Garden flower picture: 1 skein of Red Heart Super Saver Multicolor from Coats & Clark (100% acrylic; 7 oz/198 g; 364 yds/333 m) in color 310 Monet Print **4**

Lighthouse picture: 1 skein of TLC Essentials from Coats & Clark (100% acrylic; 4.5 oz/127 g; 255 yds/233 m) in color 2916 Island **4**

Fish picture: 1 skein of Red Heart Super Saver Multicolor from Coats & Clark (100% acrylic; 7 oz/198 g; 364 yds/333 m) in color 995 Ocean **4**

Notions

H-8 (5.0 mm) crochet hook or size required to obtain gauge

Assortment of decorative buttons for pictures, such as sunflowers, pansies, roses, chrysanthemums, daisies, irises, yellow butterfly, blue butterfly, ladybugs, lighthouse, sailboats, bird, fish, and seashells

Safety pins

Yarn pins

Gauge

Pullover: 12 sts and 12 rows = 4"-wide hdc patt with size H-8 hook and Light Country Blue yarn

Picture canvas: 16 sts and 17 rows = 4" puff patt with size H-8 hook and yarn for selected picture canvas

Crochet Stitches

Back single crochet (bsc), page 70; this is *not* reverse single crochet

Half double crochet (hdc), page 71

Single crochet (sc), page 70

Slip stitch (sl st), page 69

Puff Pattern

Row 1 (RS): Sc in first st and in each st across row, ch 1 (counts as 1 bsc), turn.

Row 2 (WS): Bsc in first st and in each st across, ch 1, turn.

Rep rows 1 and 2 for patt.

Wide Half Double Crochet Pattern

Row 1: Hdc in each st across, ch 2 (counts as first hdc here and throughout), turn.

Row 2: Sk first hdc in previous row, hdc in between first and second hdc of previous row. (Each hdc is

worked over horizontal warp strand between stems of hdc sts of previous row.) Work to last st, hdc in last st, ch 2, turn.

Rep row 2 for patt.

Back

- With Light Country Blue yarn, ch 38 (42, 44, 48, 50, 52, 56) sts, hdc in 3rd ch from hook and in each ch across, ch 2, turn—37 (41, 43, 47, 49, 51, 55) sts including tch.
- Beg wide hdc patt. Work even until piece measures 7 (8, 8, 8⅞, 9¾, 10¾, 10¾)". Mark this row at both ends for armhole.
- Work even until armholes measure 5⅓ (6¼, 6¼, 7⅛, 7⅛, 8, 8⅞)". Tie off.

Front

- Work as for back until armholes measure 1 (1, 1, 1, 1, 2, 2)".
- **Keyhole opening:** Change to White yarn. WORK BOTH SIDES AT SAME TIME. Work 16 (18, 19, 21, 22, 23, 25) sts. Sk next 5 sts for neck opening. With second ball of White yarn, work rem 16 (18, 19, 21, 22, 23, 25) sts.

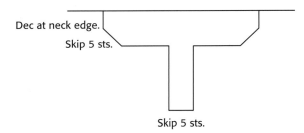

Dec at neck edge.

Skip 5 sts.

Skip 5 sts.

Keyhole neck shaping

- Work 2¾ (2¾, 3¼, 3½, 3¾, 4⅛, 4½)" even for keyhole opening.
- **Shape neck:** Sk first 5 sts at neck edge for neck shaping on side of opening. Dec 1 st at neck edge every row, until 9 (11, 12, 14, 15, 16, 18) sts rem.
- Work even until armholes measure 5⅓ (6¼, 6¼, 7⅛, 7⅛, 8, 8⅞)". Tie off.

Use your creativity to make your own fun picture scene. The four shown here are great examples of what you can do.

Sleeves (Make 2)

Sleeves are worked sideways.

- Ch 21 (21, 21, 21, 25, 25, 25) sts. Hdc in 3rd ch from hook and in ch across, ch 2, turn—20 (20, 20, 20, 24, 24, 24) sts including tch. Change to wide hdc patt.
- Work even until sleeve measures 11 (12½, 12½, 15, 15, 16, 17½)" wide. Tie off.

Picture Canvases (Make 3)

- Ch necessary number of sts needed to make picture correct size (see "Picture Directions and Materials List" below). Sc in 2nd ch from hook, sc in each st across, ch 1, turn.
- Beg with row 2 of puff patt, work in patt until picture is correct size for your creation. End after working a WS row.

- **Edging (RS):** Ch 1, sc in first st and in each st around, placing 3 sc in each corner st, sl st to ch-1. Tie off.

Large and Fancy Picture Frame

- With RS facing you, attach Gold yarn with sl st to corner of picture, ch 1, place 3 sc in the corner st, sc in each st around, cont to put 3 sc in each corner st, sl st to ch-1.
- Ch 2 (counts as hdc), *ch 1, sk next st, hdc in next st*; rep from * to * around picture, place (hdc, ch 1, hdc) in each corner st around, sl st to ch-2.
- Ch 1, sc in each st around picture, placing 3 sc in corner st of picture, sl st to ch-1.
- Ch 2, place 2 hdc in same st, (*sk 1 st, sl st in next st, 3 hdc in next st, sk 1 st*; rep from * to * around picture to corner st, place 4 hdc into corner st); rep around picture to beg, sl st to ch-2.

Picture Directions and Materials List

Garden flower picture: In color Monet Print yarn, buttons (flowers, ladybugs, butterflies), 25 sts by 23 rows. Large and fancy picture frame.

Fish picture: In color Ocean yarn, buttons (fish, seashells), 10 sts by 18 rows. Small and fancy picture frame.

Lighthouse picture: In color Island yarn, buttons (lighthouse, sailboats, bird), 20 sts by 20 rows. Basic picture frame.

Small and Fancy Picture Frame

- With RS facing you, attach 2 strands of Gold yarn with sl st to corner of picture, ch 1, place 3 sc in corner st, sc in each st around, cont to put 3 sc in each corner st, sl st to ch-1.
- Ch 2, place 2 hdc in same st, *sk next 2 sts, 3 hdc in next st*; rep from * to * around picture, placing 4 hdc into each corner st, sl st to ch-2.

Basic Frame

- With RS facing you, attach 2 strands of Gold yarn with sl st to corner st of picture, ch 1, place 3 sc in corner, sc in each st around, cont to put 3 sc in each corner st, sl st to ch-1.
- Ch 1, place 3 sc in corner st, sc in each st around, cont to put 3 sc in each corner st, sl st to ch-1.
- Ch 1, working in back lp only, place 3 sc in corner st, sc in each back lp of each st around, cont to put 3 sc in each corner st, sl st to ch-1.
- Ch 1, sl st in each st around picture. Tie off.

Finishing

- Mark center st of both front and back.
- **Seams:** With RS tog, sl st shoulders and side seams tog from bottom hem to armhole. Then with RS tog,

sl st underarm seams and sl st sleeves to armholes, easing fit. Tie off.

- **Cuff trim (for girl):** With RS facing you, attach White yarn to cuff at underarm seam. Ch 1, 2 sc in each st around arm, sl st to first st. Tie off.
- **Cuff trim (for boy):** With RS facing you, attach White yarn to cuff at underarm seam. Ch 1, 1 sc in each st around arm, sl st to first st. Tie off.
- **Bodice tails:** Attach Light Country Blue yarn to bottom-right corner of front at side seam. Working only front of bodice, work wide hdc patt for 4 rows. Inc 1 st at end of next 2 rows. Inc 1 st at both beg and end of next row. Tie off. Rep on back.
- **Bodice hem:** With RS facing you, attach yarn to bottom edge of sweater at side seam. Ch 1, sc in each st around bottom of hem, working 3 sc in each corner st and in each side seam, sl st to ch-1, tie off.
- **Neck trim:** With RS facing you, attach White yarn with sl st to shoulder seam, sc in each st around to corner of keyhole, *(sc, sl st, sc) in corner, cont with sc to next corner st*; rep from * to *, around entire neck, sl st to first sc. Tie off.
- Sew buttons onto pockets, then sew pockets and decorations to sweater.
- Weave in ends. Mist with water and lay flat to dry.

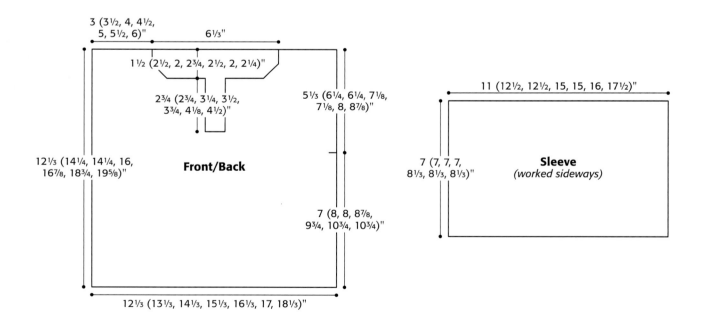

Beehive Vest

This wonderful vest will keep your busy little bee warm and comfortable in a very cozy "hive" on chilly winter mornings and cold winter nights. It can be made with or without sleeves; see page 46 for a photo with sleeves. This vest features a comfortable fit, A-line styling, and optional full-length sleeves. The beehive buttons complete the look, while the bee buttons add just the right amount of whimsy to this charming creation.

Skill Level:
Intermediate ◼◼◼▢

Size:
24 mos (2, 4, 6X, 10, 12, 14)

Child's Chest Size:
20 (22, 24, 26, 28, 30, 32)"

Finished Chest Size:
23 (25, 27, 29, 31, 33, 35)"

Finished Sleeve Length:
8 (8½, 10½, 12, 13½, 15, 16)"

Finished Body Length:
12½ (12¾, 14¾, 17, 18, 20, 22¼)"

Materials for Vest

2 (2, 2, 3, 3, 4, 4) skeins of Red Heart Plush from Coats & Clark (80% acrylic, 20% nylon; 6 oz/170 g; 290 yds/265 m) in color Apricot 9220 〔4〕

I-9 (5.5 mm) crochet hook or size required to obtain gauge for body

H-8 (5.0 mm) crochet hook or size required to obtain gauge for sleeves

4 (4, 4, 5, 5, 5, 6) beehive buttons

Assortment of decorative bee buttons, such as smiling bees, bees with folded wings, bees with open wings, and brass bees

Yarn pins

Yarn for Sleeves (Optional)

2 (2, 2, 2, 2, 3, 3) skeins of Bernat Satin from Bernat (100% acrylic; 3.5 oz/100 g; 163 yds/149 m) in color 04010 Camel 〔3〕

Gauge

Body: 8 sts and 3¾ beehive stripes = 4" in 6-CL beehive patt with size I-9 (5.5 mm) hook and Apricot yarn

Sleeves: 16 sts and 16 rows = 4" in woven patt with size H-8 (5.0 mm) hook and Camel yarn

TIP: A complete beehive stripe includes a row of cluster (CL) stitches and a row of single crochet (sc) stitches.

Crochet Stitches

6-cluster stitch (6-CL), page 73

7-cluster stitch (7-CL), page 73

Beginning cluster stitch (beg-CL), page 73

Double crochet (dc), page 71

Overstitching, page 70

Single crochet (sc), page 70

Slip stitch (sl st), page 69

Beehive Pattern (7-CL)

Row 1 (WS): Dc in first st, beg-CL st in next st, work 7-CL in each sc across to last 2 sts, beg-CL in second to last st, dc in last st, ch 1, turn.

Row 2 (RS): Sc in first st, *sk CL-closing ch-1 st, sc in next st, rep from * to end, ch 2 (does *not* count as st), turn.

Rep rows 1 and 2 for patt, ending after row 2.

Beehive Pattern (6-CL)

Row 1 (WS): Dc in first st, beg-CL in next st, work 6-CL in each sc across to last 2 sts, beg-CL in second to last st, dc in last st, ch 1, turn.

Row 2 (RS): Sc in first st, *sk CL-closing ch-1 st, sc in next st, rep from * to end, ch 2 (does *not* count as st), turn.

Rep rows 1 and 2 for patt, ending after row 2.

Woven Pattern (Collar and Optional Sleeves)

This pattern must be worked on an even number of stitches.

Row 1: Ch 1, sc in first st, ch 1, *sk next st, sc in next st, ch 1*; rep * to * to last st, sc in last st, turn.

Row 2: Ch 1, sc in first st, *ch 1, sk next st, sc in ch-1 sp*; rep * to * to last st, sc in last st, turn.

Rep row 2 for patt.

Body

- **Work as 1 piece:** With size I-9 hook and Apricot yarn, ch 53 (59, 63, 67, 71, 76, 79). Sc in 2nd ch from hook and in each ch across—52 (58, 62, 66, 70, 75, 78) sts. Mark this as RS with safety pin. Ch 2 (does *not* count as st), turn.

- **Beg hem:** Dc in first st, work beg-CL in each st across to last st, dc in last st, ch 1, turn.

NOTE: This row will fan out because you added one stitch for each cluster in the row. This is OK. The next row will decrease one stitch for each cluster.

- Sc in first st, *sk ch-1 st, sc in next st*; rep from * to last st, sc in last st, ch 1, turn.

- **Turning row:** Sc in first st and in each st across, ch 2, turn.

- **Next row (RS):** Dc in first st, work beg-CL in second st, then work 7-CL in each rem st across to last 2 sts, work beg-CL in next st, dc in last st, ch 1, turn.

- **Next row (WS):** Sc in first st and in each st across, ch 2, turn.

- Fold beg-CL row up level with 7-CL row just completed. *Remember that RS of 7-CL row is RS of bodice.* Sc2tog first st of 7-CL row to first sc of first row, *sk CL-closing ch-1 st in current row, sc2tog next st of 7-CL row with next sc of beg-CL row*; rep from * to * to end of row, ch 2, turn. This folded row will be considered as first CL row in directions below.

- **Beg A-line shaping:** Beg with CL row, work beehive patt (7-CL) for 2 more beehive stripes, dec 1 st at beg and end of each CL row.

- Change to beehive patt (6-CL), dec 1 st at beg, end, and in middle of every CL row until 43 (47, 51, 55, 59, 63, 67) sts rem.

*NOTE: Decrease in cluster rows **only**.*

- Work even until 4 (5, 6, 7, 8, 9, 10) beehive stripes have been completed. Body should measure approx 6¼ (5⅓, 6⅓, 7½, 8½, 9½, 10½)". Work additional rows if necessary to achieve correct length. End after working a RS sc row.

- Split piece into 3 sections as follows:

- **Right front (WS):** Beg with CL row, work beehive patt (6-CL) over first 10 (11, 12, 13, 14, 15, 16) sts only. Work beehive patt (6-CL) until armhole has

3 (4, 4, 4, 5, 5, 6) beehive stripes completed. Armhole should measure approx 4¼ (4½, 5½, 6½, 6½, 7½, 9½)". Work additional rows if necessary to achieve correct length.

- **Shape neck (WS):** On neck edge of next CL-row, sl st first 2 (2, 3, 3, 3, 3, 4) sts on neck edge and cont beehive patt (6-CL). Beg with next CL-row, dec 1 st at neck edge (right end) every CL-row, until 6 (7, 8, 8, 8, 9, 10) sts rem.
- Work piece even until armhole has 6 (7, 8, 9, 9, 10, 11) beehive stripes completed. Armhole should measure approx 6⅓ (7½, 8½, 9½, 9½, 10½, 11½)". Work additional rows if necessary to achieve correct length. Tie off.
- **Back (RS):** Work even over next 23 (25, 27, 29, 31, 33, 35) sts until armhole has 7 (8, 9, 10, 10, 11, 12) beehive stripes completed. Armhole should measure approx 6⅓ (7½, 8½, 9½, 9½, 10½, 11½)". Work additional rows if necessary to achieve correct length. Tie off.
- **Left front:** Work over rem 10 (11, 12, 13, 14, 15, 16) sts. Work as for right front, beg neck shaping on WS sc row and working decs at left end of piece on CL rows.

Armholes

- **Shoulder seams:** With RS tog, sl st fronts to back at shoulder seams. Tie off.
- **Armhole trim:** With WS facing you and using size I-9 hook, attach Apricot yarn to bottom of an armhole with sl st, ch 1, sc evenly around armhole, (be sure to

place 2 sc in each CL row). To prevent holes between trim and vest, make 1 sc around dc and sc which is stretched to attach to CL st next to dc, cont around armhole. Sl st to ch-1.

- Sl st in each sc st around armhole, ch 1 to beg sl st. Tie off.
- Attach Apricot yarn at bottom of armhole and under lip of armhole trim with sl st ½" from edge (see illustration on page 70).
- Using overstitching, ch 1, sc evenly around inside of armhole, sl st to ch-1. This will be connection for optional sleeve. Rep on 2nd armhole.

Finishing

- **Trim:** With RS facing you, attach Apricot yarn to bottom of right front with sl st, ch 1, sc evenly up front, being sure to place 2 sc in each CL row. To prevent holes between trim and vest, make 1 sc around dc st and sc which is stretched to attach to CL st next to dc, cont around neck, placing sc in each sc, to center st, place 2 sc in center st, cont around neck and down other side. Sl st to ch-1, ch 1, turn.
- Sc in first st and in each st around neck and lapels. Tie off.
- **Buttonhole band (RS):** *Right front* for girl, *left front* for boy. Attach Apricot yarn to bottom (girl) or top (boy) corner of front at neck with sl st. Sc in each st across band, ch 1, turn. Mark the position of one button 1" from top edge and another button 1½" from bottom edge. Evenly space remaining buttons between these two.

- (Sc in each st to position marked for button, ch 2, sk next 2 sts); rep until all buttonholes are made, and then sc in each rem st to end of band, ch 1, turn.

- (Sc in each st to buttonhole, place 2 sc around the ch-2 sp); rep until all buttonholes are finished, sc in each st to end, ch 1, turn.

- Sc in each st across buttonhole band, around neck, and along other front edge. Tie off.

- **Button band (RS):** *Left front* for girl, *right front* for boy. Attach Apricot yarn to top (girl) or bottom (boy) corner of front with sl st. (Sc in each st across front, ch 1, turn); rep 2 more times. Cont to sc in each st around neck, working 2 sc in each shoulder seam, to top of other button band. Tie off.

- **Trim around fronts and neck (RS):** Attach Apricot yarn to bottom of button or buttonhole band where it attaches to body, sl st in each st across button-band bottom, working (sl st, ch 1, sl st) in corner, and then 1 sl st in each st up button band, around neck, and down buttonhole band and working (sl st, ch 1, sl st) in corner, sl st in each st across bottom of button band to body. Tie off.

- Sew beehive buttons at marked positions on button band, being careful to align buttons with buttonholes. Tie off.

- Randomly arrange remaining decorative bee buttons and sew to sweater.

Optional Sleeves (Make 2)

Sleeves are joined to the shoulder and then worked in the round to the cuff. Each round is joined and then turned as if worked in rows.

- With RS facing you and using size H-8 hook, attach Camel yarn to underside of armhole trim with a sl st. Ch 1, sc evenly around armhole to underside of trim, sl st to ch-1.

NOTE: Count your stitches and record the number for crocheting the second sleeve. Make sure you have an even number of stitches.

- Ch 1, beg woven patt, working in the round, remembering to sl st to ch-1 to join each rnd before turning. Dec 1 st at each end of every 4 rows, until 28 (28, 30, 32, 32, 34, 36) sts rem. Work even until sleeve measures 8 (8½, 10½, 12, 13½, 15, 16)". Tie off.

- Weave in ends. Mist with water and lay flat to dry.

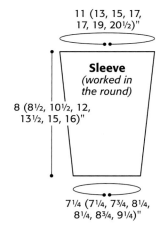

11 (13, 15, 17, 17, 19, 20½)"

Sleeve
(worked in the round)

8 (8½, 10½, 12, 13½, 15, 16)"

7¼ (7¼, 7¾, 8¼, 8¼, 8¾, 9¼)"

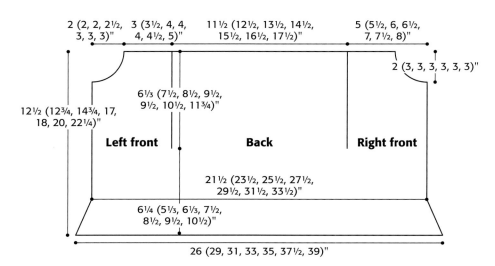

2 (2, 2, 2½, 3, 3, 3)" 3 (3½, 4, 4, 4, 4½, 5)" 11½ (12½, 13½, 14½, 15½, 16½, 17½)" 5 (5½, 6, 6½, 7, 7½, 8)"

2 (3, 3, 3, 3, 3, 3)"

6⅓ (7½, 8½, 9½, 9½, 10½, 11¾)"

12½ (12¾, 14¾, 17, 18, 20, 22¼)"

Left front　**Back**　**Right front**

21½ (23½, 25½, 27½, 29½, 31½, 33½)"

6¼ (5⅓, 6⅓, 7½, 8½, 9½, 10½)"

26 (29, 31, 33, 35, 37½, 39)"

Birdhouse Cardigan

The family's little bird lover will enjoy the birdhouse buttons on this rustic creation. This cardigan is lightweight and perfect for a late fall or early spring stroll in a park, or for just cuddling on the couch in the living room and watching the birds outside. If you don't have one, consider purchasing a bird feeder so that your little one can watch the birds come and go. You might even get your little sweetheart out of bed in the morning without the constant strife if she knows she can wear her "bird-watching" sweater and watch the birds eat their breakfast. The cardigan is collarless and has a V-neck. It is waist-length and has a straight body, two-tone body hem, drop shoulder, and full-length sleeves. If you wish, add bird buttons to the front of the sweater for more fun.

Skill Level:
Intermediate ◼◼◼▢

Size:
24 mos (2, 4, 6X, 10, 12, 14)

Child's Chest Size:
20 (22, 24, 26, 28, 30, 32)"

Finished Chest Size:
26 (27¾, 30, 32½, 34¼, 36½, 38¾)"

Finished Sleeve Length:
8½ (9, 11, 12½, 14, 15½, 16½)"

Finished Body Length:
11½ (12½, 13½, 14½, 16½, 17½, 18½)"

Materials

2 (3, 3, 3, 4, 4, 4) skeins of Wool-Ease from Lion Brand Yarn (86% acrylic, 10% wool, 4% rayon; 3 oz/85 g; 197 yds/180 m) in color Mink Brown 127 [4]

1 skein of Wool-Ease from Lion Brand Yarn (80% acrylic, 20% wool; 3 oz/85 g; 197 yds/180 m) in color Forest Green Heather 180 [4]

1 skein of Caron Simply Soft Brites from Caron International (100% acrylic; 6 oz/170 g; 330 yds) in color Berry Blue 9609 [4]

J-10 (6.0 mm) crochet hook or size required to obtain gauge

3 (3, 3, 4, 4, 4, 4) birdhouse buttons

Assortment of decorative bird buttons, such as blue jays and cardinals

Safety pins

Gauge

13.5 sts and 7 rows = 4" in wooden slat patt with size J-10 hook and Mink Brown yarn

Crochet Stitches

Back-stitch double crochet (BSdc), page 74; this is *not* back-post double crochet

Double crochet (dc), page 71

Front-stitch double crochet (FSdc), page 73; this is *not* front-post double crochet

Half double crochet (hdc), page 71

Single crochet (sc), page 70

Slip stitch (sl st), page 69

Wooden Slat Pattern

Row 1 (WS): FSdc around first st and around each st across, dc into top ch of ch-3 from previous row, ch 3 (counts as first dc now and throughout), turn.

Row 2 (RS): BSdc around first st and around each st across, dc into top ch of ch-3 from previous row, ch 3 (counts as first dc now and throughout), turn.

Rep rows 1 and 2 for patt. Take care to count sts to be sure you don't lose or add sts.

NOTE: Remember to end every row with a regular double crochet.

Body

- **Work as 1 piece (RS):** With Mink Brown yarn, ch 87 (93, 101, 109, 115, 123, 131) sts, dc in 4th ch from hook, dc in each st across, ch 3 (counts as first dc now and throughout), turn—85 (91, 99, 107, 113, 121, 129) sts including tch.
- Work wooden slat patt until piece measures 4 (5, 6, 6, 7, 8, 8)".
- Split piece into 3 sections as follows:
- **Right front:** Work patt over first 21 (23, 24, 27, 28, 30, 32) sts only, cont wooden slat patt.
- **Shape neck:** At neck edge, dec 1 st every row, until 11 (13, 14, 17, 18, 20, 22) sts rem.
- Cont to work piece even until armhole measures 6 (6, 6, 7, 8, 8, 9)". Tie off.

- **Back:** Work over next 42 (44, 50, 52, 56, 60, 64) sts only being sure to match the wooden slat patt of right front. Work back of piece even until armhole measures 6 (6, 6, 7, 8, 8, 9)". Tie off.
- **Left front:** Work piece over rem 22 (24, 25, 28, 29, 31, 33) sts. Work as for right front, being careful to work decs at neck edge for V-neck shaping. Tie off.
- **Sew shoulder seams:** With WS tog, sl st front to back at shoulder seams. Tie off.

Sleeves (Make 2)

Sleeves are worked sideways to match the nap of the pattern. The center of the sleeve is worked first, and then side shaping.

- With Mink Brown yarn, ch 29 (30, 37, 42, 47, 52, 56) sts, dc in 4th ch from hook and in each ch across, ch 2, turn—27 (28, 35, 40, 45, 50, 54) sts including tch.
- Count number of slats around armhole formed in bodice. Subtract 6 from number. Cont with wooden slat patt until number of slats for sleeve equals number of slats around armhole minus 6. End after working a WS row.
- **Beg sleeve shaping (RS):** Cont with row 2 of wooden slat patt to 8 sts from end of sleeve. Hdc in next st, sc in next st, sl st in next 2 sts, ch 2, turn.
- Sk first st, sl st in each of next 9 sts, placing marker on 9th sl st, sc in next st, hdc in next st, cont with row 1 of wooden slat patt to end of row, turn.

- Ch 1, sc in same st, sc in each of next 2 sts, *sk next st, sc in next 3 sts*, rep from * to * around wrist, sl st to ch-1 st.
- Ch 1, sl st in each st around wrist, sl st to ch-1 st. Tie off.
- Rep cuff trim on second sleeve.

Finishing

- **Bodice trim:** With RS facing you, attach Berry Blue yarn to bottom corner with sl st, ch 1, sc in first st and in each st across, ch 1, turn.
- Sc in first st and in each st across. Tie off.
- Attach Forest Green Heather yarn with sl st to bottom corner, ch 1, turn.
- Sc in first st and in each st across, ch 1, turn.
- Ch 1 (ch 1 counts as first sc here and throughout), dc in next st, *sc, dc*, rep * to * to end, ch 1, turn.
- Sc in first st and in each st across, ch 1, turn.
- Sc in first st and in each st across, ch 1, turn.
- Ch 1, dc in next st, *sc, dc*, rep * to * to end, ch 1, turn. Tie off.
- **Button and buttonhole bands:** With RS facing you, attach Mink Brown yarn to lower-right front, ch 1, sc in first st and in each st up front, around neck and down left front, ch 1, turn.
- Sc in first st and in each st up left front, place 2 sc in corner st which separates front from V-neck, cont around neck, place 2 sc in corner st which separates front from V-neck, cont down right front, ch 1, turn.
- Sc in first st and in each st up right front, around neck, down left front, ch 1, turn.

For Boy Version Only

- **Buttonhole band (left front):** Mark positions for buttons, placing first one ½" from bottom and last one ½" from top, and spacing rest evenly between these 2 positions. (Sc in each st to position marked for button, ch 3, sk next 3 sts, sc in next st); rep until all buttonholes are made, then sc in each rem st to top of left front band, ch 1, turn. Sc in each sc down left front band. Tie off.
- **Button band (right front):** With RS facing you, attach Mink Brown yarn to lower-right front, ch 1, sc in first st and in each st up right front only, ch 1, turn. Sc in each sc down right front band only, ch 1, turn.

- Cont with row 2 of wooden slat patt to 8 sts before marker. Hdc in next st, sc in next st, sl st in next 2. Tie off.
- With WS facing you, attach yarn to shoulder end of sleeve on straight side. Cont with row 1 of wooden slat patt to 8 sts from end of sleeve. Hdc in next st, sc in next st, sl st in next 2 sts, ch 2, turn.
- Sk first st, sl st in each of next 9 sts, placing marker on 9th sl st, sc in next st, hdc in next st, cont with row 1 of wooden slat patt to end of row, turn.
- Cont with row 2 of wooden slat patt to 8 sts before marker. Hdc in next st, sc in next st, sl st in next 2. Do not tie off.
- **Sew sleeve seam:** With WS of sleeve tog, sl st in each st across sleeve. Tie off.
- **Sew sleeves into armholes:** Place RS of sleeve to RS of bodice, being sure to place seam of sleeve at bottom of armhole and match segment to segment around armhole. Sl st pieces tog in each st of armhole.
- **Cuff trim:** With RS facing you, attach Mink Brown yarn to wrist of sleeve, ch 1, sc in same st, sc evenly around wrist, sl st to ch-1 st.

For Girl Version Only

- **Button band (left front):** Sc in each sc up left front band only, ch 1, turn.
- Sc in each sc down left front band. Tie off.
- **Buttonhole band (right front):** Mark positions for buttons, placing first one ½" from bottom and last one ½" from top, and spacing rest evenly between these 2 positions. With RS facing you, attach Mink Brown yarn to lower-right front, (sc in each st to position marked for button, ch 3, sk next 3 sts, sc in next st); rep until all buttonholes are made, then sc in each rem st to top of right front band, ch 1, turn. Sc in each sc down right front band, ch 1, turn.

For Both Boy and Girl Versions

- Sc in each sc up right front band, (sc, ch 1, sc) in corner st, cont around neck, (sc, ch 1, sc) in corner st, cont down left front band. Tie off.
- Sew birdhouse buttons at marked positions on button band, being careful to align buttonholes with buttons.
- Randomly arrange remaining decorative bird buttons and sew to sweater.
- Weave in ends. Mist with water and lay flat to dry.

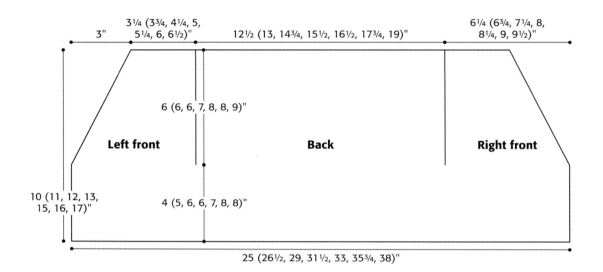

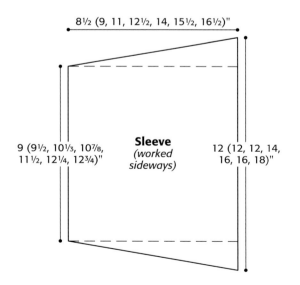

Blue Duck Cardigan

Isn't this the perfect sweater for a baby boy or that baby girl you just know will be a little tomboy? This creation is a waist-length, straight-bodied cardigan with drop shoulders and grafted, full-length, straight sleeves. The sweater has a comfortable fit for ease when dressing your little one.

Skill Level:
Easy ◼◼◻◻

Size:
18 mos (24 mos, 2)

Child's Chest Size:
24 lbs (22, 24)"

Finished Chest Size:
26 (23½, 26)"

Finished Sleeve Length:
7 (7¾, 8¼)"

Finished Body Length:
10 (10½, 11½)"

Materials

3 (3, 4) skeins of Snuggly DK from Sirdar (55% nylon, 45% acrylic; 50 g; 191 yds/175 m) in color Pastel Blue 321 ③

F-6 (4.0 mm) crochet hook or size required to obtain gauge

4 blue duck buttons

Gauge

18 sts and 11 rows = 4" in body patt with size F-6 (4.0 mm) hook

Crochet Stitches

Double crochet (dc), page 71

Half double crochet (hdc), page 71

Single crochet (sc), page 70

Slip stitch (sl st), page 69

Body Pattern

Worked over a multiple of 6 sts.

Row 1 (RS): Work in back lps only, sc in first st, *hdc in next st, sc in next st*, rep from * to * to last st, hdc, ch 2 (count as hdc in this row and in following rows), turn.

Row 2: Hdc in 2nd st, *sc in next st, hdc in next st*, rep from * to * across, ch 1, turn.

Row 3: Sc in first st, *hdc in next st, sc in next st*, rep from * to * to last st, hdc in last st, ch 1, turn.

Row 4: Sc in each st across, ch 1, turn.

Row 5: Working in back lps only, sc in each st across, ch 3 (count as dc in this row and following rows), turn.

Row 6: Dc in 2nd st and each st across, ch 3, turn.

Row 7: Dc in 2nd st, *ch 1, sk next st, dc in each of next 2 sts*, rep from * to * across to last st, dc in tch, ch 3, turn.

Row 8: Dc in 2nd st and in each dc and ch sp across to last st, dc in tch, ch 3, turn.

Row 9: Rep row 7.

Row 10: Dc in 2nd st and in each dc and ch sp across, ch 1, turn.

Rep rows 1–10 for patt.

Sleeve Pattern (Worked in the Round)

Rnd 1: Ch 1, working in back lps only, sc in first st and in each st around, sl st to ch-1.

Rnd 2: Ch 3 (counts as dc in this and following rnds), dc in each st around, sl st to ch-3.

Rnd 3: Ch 3, dc in next st, *ch 1, sk next st, dc in next 2 sts, * rep from * to * to last st, dc in last st, sl st to ch-3.

NOTE: Always double crochet in last stitch of round 3 even if you have to leave out a chain space.

Rnd 4: Ch 3, dc in each st and ch sp around armhole, sl st to ch 3.

Rep rnds 1–4 for patt.

Body

• **Work as 1 piece:** Ch 115 (103, 115) loosely, using a larger hook if necessary. Sc in 2nd ch from hook and in each st across—114 (102, 114) sc. Ch 3 (counts as 1 dc), turn.

• Dc in 2nd st and in each st across, ch 1, turn.

• Sc in first st and in each st across, ch 1, turn.

• **Beg body patt (RS):** Work even until piece measures 3⅝ (5, 4½)". End after working a WS row.

• Split piece into 3 sections as follows:

• **Right front (RS):** Cont body patt over first 28 (26, 28) sts only, and work even until armhole measures 3⅝".

• **Shape neck (WS):** Work over 22 (20, 22) sts. Turn, skipping last 5 (6, 6) sts for front neck. Beg on next row, dec 1 st at neck edge (right end) every row, until 16 (18, 16) sts rem.

• Work body patt even until armhole measures 5¾ (5¾, 6½)". Tie off.

• **Back (RS):** Work over next 58 (50, 58) sts only, cont body patt to match right front.

• Work even until armhole measures 5¾ (5, 6½)". Tie off.

• **Left front (RS):** Work over rem 28 (26, 28) sts. Work as for right front, beg neck shaping on RS row and working decs on left end of piece. Tie off.

• **Shoulder seams:** With RS tog, sl st fronts to back at shoulder seams. Tie off.

Sleeves (Make 2)

Sleeves are joined to the shoulder and then worked in the round to the cuff.

• Ch 1, sc in first st and in each st around armhole, sl st to ch-1.

NOTE: Count your stitches and record the number for crocheting the second sleeve.

- Ch 1, working in back lps only, hdc in first st, *sc in next st, hdc in next st*; rep from * to * across, sl st to ch-1.
- Ch 2, working in both lps, 1 sc in first st, *hdc, sc*; rep from * to * across, sl st to ch-2 (dec 1 st in this rnd).
- Ch 1, working in both lps, 1 hdc in next st, *sc in next st, hdc in next st*; rep from * to * across, sl st to ch-1.
- Work in sleeve patt, dec 1 st in row 2 until 39 (42, 44) sts rem. Work even in patt until sleeve measures 6¼ (7, 7⅝)" long. Tie off.

Finishing

- **Sleeve trim:** With RS facing you, attach yarn to cuff. Ch 1, working in back lps only sc in first st and in each st around, sl st to ch-1.
- (Ch 1, working in both lps, sc in first st and in each st around, sl st to ch-1); rep 2 more times. Tie off.
- **Buttonhole band:** *Right front* for girl, *left front* for boy. With RS facing you, attach yarn to bottom right (girl) or top left (boy) front of cardigan with sl st, sc evenly across band, ch 1, turn.
- Sc in each st of band, ch 1, turn.
- Mark positions for 4 buttonholes, placing first one ¼" from bottom and last one ¼" from top, and spacing rest evenly between these 2 positions.
- (Sc in each st to position marked for button, ch 2, sk next 2 sts, sc in next st); rep until all buttonholes are

made, then sc in each rem st to bottom of band, ch 1, turn.
- (Sc in each st to buttonhole, place 2 sc around ch-2 sp); rep until all buttonholes are finished, sc in each st to end of band, ch 1, turn.
- Sc in each st of band. Tie off.
- **Button band:** *Left front* for girl, *right front* for boy. With RS facing you, attach yarn to top left (girl) or bottom right (boy) front with sl st, sc evenly across band, ch 1, turn.
- (Sc in each st of band, ch 1, turn); rep 4 more times. Tie off.
- Sew buttons at marked positions on button band, being careful to align buttons with buttonholes.
- **Body trim:** With RS facing you, attach yarn to lower corner of cardigan front. Ch 1, sc in each st up band, around neck, down opposite band and along bottom, sl st to ch-1.
- (Ch 1, sc in each st around sweater as in previous step); rep once more.
- Weave in ends. Mist with water and lay flat to dry.

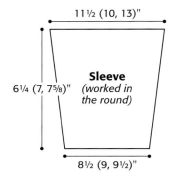

11½ (10, 13)"

6¼ (7, 7⅝)"

Sleeve
(worked in the round)

8½ (9, 9½)"

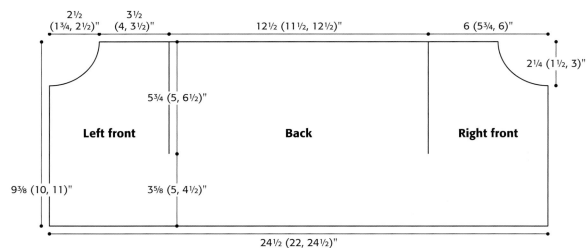

2½ (1¾, 2½)"   3½ (4, 3½)"   12½ (11½, 12½)"   6 (5¾, 6)"

2¼ (1½, 3)"

5¾ (5, 6½)"

Left front   **Back**   **Right front**

9⅜ (10, 11)"   3⅝ (5, 4½)"

24½ (22, 24½)"

Updated Renaissance Serf Tunic

This colorful rendition of a Renaissance tunic will brighten the day of your own little "serfs." Who knows, you may even be able to get some work out of them—like picking up the games, dolls, and cars in their rooms! Well, at least you can dream.

This unisex tunic has a moderate fit with full sleeves, a straight body, and a keyhole front collar. The tunic also features contrasting trim. This is the perfect project to make if you're just starting out making crocheted sweaters.

Skill Level:
Beginner ■□□□

Size:
24 mos (2, 4, 6X, 10, 12, 14)

Child's Chest Size:
20 (22, 24, 26, 28, 30, 32)"

Finished Chest Size:
23¼ (24½, 27¼, 28½, 30, 34, 35¼)"

Finished Sleeve Length:
8½ (9, 11¼, 13, 14½, 16½, 17½)"

Finished Body Length:
15 (15¾, 17, 18½, 20, 21¾, 21¾)"
including tails

Materials

2 (2, 3, 3, 4, 4, 4) skeins of Caron Simply Soft Brites from Caron International (100% acrylic; 6 oz/170 g; 330 yds) in color Mango 9605 **4**

1 skein of Caron Simply Soft Brites from Caron International (100% acrylic; 6 oz/170 g; 330 yds) in color Limelight 9607 **4**

1 skein of Suede Yarn from Lion Brand Yarn (100% polyester; 85 g/3 oz; 122 yds/10 m) in color Ecru 210 **5**

H-8 (5.0 mm) crochet hook or size required to obtain gauge

J-10 (6.0 mm) crochet hook for foundation chains

Yarn pins

Gauge

12 sts and 10 rows = 4" in wide hdc patt with size H-8 (5.0 mm) hook and Mango yarn

Crochet Stitches

Half double crochet (hdc), page 71

Single crochet (sc), page 70

Slip stitch (sl st), page 69

Reverse single crochet (rsc), page 71

Wide Half Double Crochet Pattern

Row 1: Hdc in each st across, ch 2 (counts as first hdc here and throughout), turn.

Row 2: Sk first hdc in previous row, hdc in between first and second hdc of previous row. (Each hdc is worked over horizontal warp strand between stems of hdc sts of previous row.) Work to the last st, hdc in last st, ch 2, turn.

Rep row 2 for patt.

Back

- With size J-10 hook and Mango yarn, ch 36 (38, 42, 44, 46, 52, 54). Switch to size H-8 hook, hdc in 3rd ch from hook and in each st across, ch 2, turn—35 (37, 41, 43, 45, 51, 53) sts including tch.
- **Beg wide hdc patt.** Work even until piece measures 6¾ (6¾, 8, 8¾, 9¾, 10¾, 10)". End after working a WS row.
- **Beg sleeves (RS):** At opposite edge of bodice from original skein of yarn, attach another skein of yarn, ch 26 (27, 34, 39, 44, 50, 53) sts. Tie off second skein of yarn.
- With original skein of yarn at edge of bodice, ch 28 (29, 36, 41, 46, 52, 55) sts. Hdc in 3rd ch from hook, hdc in each ch to bodice, at bodice edge cont with wide hdc patt to other edge of bodice. Hdc in each st of ch to end of ch, ch 2, turn.

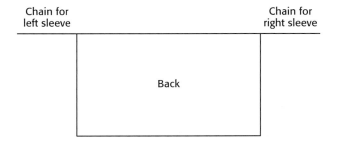

- Cont with wide hdc patt, working even until armhole measures 5⅓ (6, 6, 6¾, 7⅓, 8, 8¾)". Tie off.

Front

- Work as for back to one row after beg sleeves.
- **Keyhole opening (RS):** Work over first 43 (45, 54, 60, 67, 75, 79) sts only. With second skein of yarn attach with sl st to next st at center, ch 2, hdc in same sp cont working wide hdc patt over rem sts.
- Cont wide hdc pattern WORKING BOTH SIDES OF FRONT AT SAME TIME until keyhole opening measures 2½ (2¾, 2¾, 3¾, 4, 4¼, 5½)".
- **Shape neck:** For bottom of neckline, sk first 5 sts at neck edge. Beg on next row, dec 1 st at neck edge every row until 35 (36, 45, 51, 58, 66, 70) sts rem.
- Work even until sleeve measures 5⅓ (6, 6, 6¾, 7⅓, 8, 8¾)". Do not tie off. Use this yarn to sl st shoulder seams tog. (One less knot!)

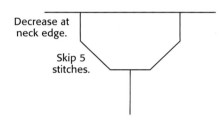

Decrease at neck edge.

Skip 5 stitches.

Join second skein of yarn and work left and right front separately.

Keyhole neck shaping

Finishing

- **Seams:** With RS tog, pin front and back tog with yarn pins at shoulders. Sl st fronts to back at shoulder seams.
- With RS tog, sl st underarm and side seams.
- **Tunic tails:** With RS facing you, attach Mango yarn to bottom of front at side seam with sl st, ch 2, cont with wide hdc patt, working only on front. Inc by 1 st at each row of flap until tunic measures 15 (15¾, 17, 18½, 20, 21¾, 21¾)". Tie off. Rep tunic tail on back.
- **Trim (RS):** Attach Mango yarn to neck with sl st, ch 1, sc in each st around neck being sure to even out steps around neck to achieve rounded neck. Tie off. Attach Limelight yarn, ch 1, rsc in each sc around neck. Tie off. Rep trim on sleeve cuffs and at bottom of tunic.
- **Ties:** With RS facing, attach Suede yarn with sl st to one side of bottom neck slot, ch 4, sl st to other side of neck slot to attach ch. Ch 5, sl st to other side, straight across. Ch 5, sl st to other side diagonally down to original start, cut yarn with long tail. Bring crochet hook and yarn to WS of sweater, sl st to original sl st. Tie off.
- Weave in ends. Mist with water and lay flat to dry.

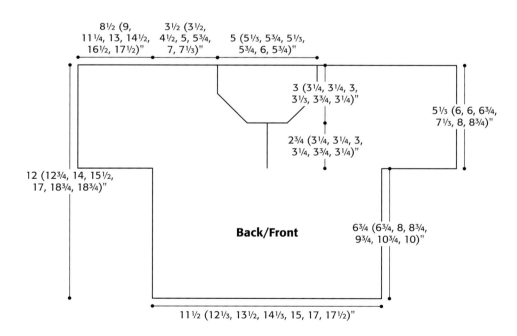

8½ (9, 11¼, 13, 14½, 16½, 17½)"

3½ (3½, 4½, 5, 5¾, 7, 7⅓)"

5 (5⅓, 5¾, 5⅓, 5¾, 6, 5¾)"

3 (3¼, 3¼, 3, 3⅓, 3¾, 3¼)"

5⅓ (6, 6, 6¾, 7⅓, 8, 8¾)"

2¾ (3¼, 3¼, 3, 3¼, 3¾, 3¼)"

12 (12¾, 14, 15½, 17, 18¾, 18¾)"

Back/Front

6¾ (6¾, 8, 8¾, 9¾, 10¾, 10)"

11½ (12⅓, 13½, 14⅓, 15, 17, 17½)"

Yarn Basics for Crochet

I am often asked what my favorite type of yarn is. Do I prefer wool, cotton, or acrylic fibers? Well, for the record, I have always preferred the yarn that is on sale. I just can't resist a good bargain. Nor have I ever been able to resist the balls, skeins, or shanks of yarn that are just sitting dejectedly on a shelf waiting for a good home. I have a big heart! I just wish my wallet were as big. The following section covers the yarn basics for crochet, including weights, fiber content, dye lots, and drape.

Yarn Weights

Yarn manufacturers prefer to categorize yarn by weight instead of by thickness because the weight of a skein of yarn is easier to measure than the yarn's thickness. A skein or shank of worsted-weight yarn is heavier than a skein of sport-weight or fingering-weight yarn with the same yardage.

Yarn-Weight Chart

The following yarn-weight chart was developed by the Craft Yarn Council of America.

Yarn-Weight Symbol and Category Names	1 SUPER FINE	2 FINE	3 LIGHT	4 MEDIUM	5 BULKY	6 SUPER BULKY
Types of Yarns in Category	Sock, Fingering, Baby	Sport, Baby	DK, Light Worsted	Worsted, Afghan, Aran	Chunky, Craft, Rug	Bulky, Roving
Crochet Gauge Ranges in Single Crochet to 4"	21 to 32 sts	16 to 20 sts	12 to 17 sts	11 to 14 sts	8 to 11 sts	5 to 9 sts
Recommended Hook in Metric Size Range	2.25 to 3.5 mm	3.5 to 4.5 mm	4.5 to 5.5 mm	5.5 to 6.5 mm	6.5 to 9 mm	9 mm and larger
Recommended Hook in U.S. Size Range	B-1 to E-4	E-4 to 7	7 to I-9	I-9 to K-10½	K-10½ to M-13	M-13 and larger

Conversion Chart

m	= yds	x	0.9144
yds	= m	x	1.0936
g	= oz	x	28.35
oz	= g	x	0.0352

Yarn Fibers

Wool and wool blends are among my favorite types of yarns. These yarns are great for apparel items, afghans, and household items like tea cozies. The new super-wash wool yarns are great for clothing for kids because they go in the washing machine just like an acrylic.

Silk and silk blends are among my luxurious favorites. These yarns are best worked with wood or bamboo crochet hooks to inhibit excessive sliding along the shaft of the hook. The premium price of these yarns will be worth every penny when you slip into them. However, do take great care with tying knots with these types of yarns because the strands easily slide past each other. (Translation: These yarns are slippery little rascals and allow knots to come undone.) You may want to try a square knot when tying off, and weave the tails of the knot into the fabric right away to limit their desire to unravel.

Acrylics and acrylic blends are great yarns for beginners and are excellent choices for clothing, afghans, and children's apparel. The greatest strengths of these yarns are their price, variety, wide availability, and easy washing requirements. It's unfortunate that a lot of snubbing of these yarns has developed over the years in the crocheting and knitting worlds. This prejudice was the result of the old acrylic yarns and their low quality. However, today's acrylic yarns are wonderful and deserve more respect than they currently receive. Try them out. You won't regret it.

Nylon and nylon blends are the traditional fibers used for macramé. Macramé generally will combine nylon threads to form cords, and then the cords are used to make projects. However, there are finer crochet threads and some very beautiful yarns produced from this material. The nicest feature of nylon yarns is that nylon doesn't absorb water like a cotton or wool. Hence, it's the material of choice for making swim outfits, outdoor clothing, and camping equipment like tents. It also washes up very well, which makes the yarn great for children's clothing as well.

Alpaca wool is 50% warmer than sheep's wool. It's generally a premium yarn that is best left to intermediate or experienced crocheters. The projects made from this yarn can only be dry-cleaned, unless you're trying to achieve a felted texture, in which case you cold wash them. But remember—a felted texture must also be made with an appropriately sized pattern because the shrinkage is significant. I have only used this yarn to make very special projects but I love working with it!

Novelty yarns can be nylon, acrylic, cotton, or wool blends. Although these can be tricky for the brand-new beginner, an advanced beginner can usually handle these types of yarns. The important thing to remember about these yarns is that they may require special washing. Since they are usually combined with other yarn types, you need to know whether the other yarns they're combined with will shrink more than the novelty yarns. If so, you may need to preshrink the item before adding the novelty yarns if possible. It's best when starting with novelty yarn to find a pattern that calls for this yarn rather than trying to use it as a substitute yarn in a pattern. The designer of the pattern will have taken

into consideration the lack of stretch in these yarns and differences in shrinking percentages.

Cotton is the most common and traditional material used for crochet thread. Look for mercerized cotton when using this type of thread. Mercerized cotton is treated with alkali, which improves the luster and strength of the cotton. The crochet threads show off intricate patterns beautifully and are perfect for summer apparel, curtains, bedspreads, doilies, and kitchen projects. Unmercerized cotton yarn is softer and may be a good choice for kids' clothing too.

Linen threads make very fine and delicate, yet unbelievably strong fabrics. If you have a project with a delicate mesh-type or lacy pattern, this thread may be just the thing. The fine threads show off intricate patterns beautifully and are great for summer apparel, curtains, bedspreads, and doilies.

Do You Believe You're Allergic to Wool?

Most people are *sensitive* to wool rather than *allergic*. People who are sensitive to wool react to the fine, sharp sheath that surrounds the wool fiber. The new "non-itch" wools remove this sheath, making the wool itch-free. I know this because I am susceptible to rashes with old-fashioned wools, but the new wools don't bother me at all. However, my friend Colleen is truly allergic to wool. Her skin doesn't break out as mine does, but her throat closes up when she tries to wear wool. So, if wool just makes you itch, then give the non-itch wools a try. However, if you're allergic to wool, then you'll have to content yourself with the polyester, nylon, silk, and new acrylic yarns, which you'll find to be absolutely wonderful.

Dye Lots

A dye lot is a batch number for coloring yarn. It's necessary when the yarn manufacturers or dyers make relatively small batches of color. The color in different batches, or dye lots, will be similar but not exact, so it is very important that you buy enough yarn from the same dye lot to complete a project. You'll notice some companies have yarns with a "no dye lot" designation. This is possible because of the new dyes available today and the computer control over the dyeing process. Most brands of yarn keep the color fairly consistent, so if you run out, always take some yarn with you to the store, along with the dye lot number. You can often get lucky and find the same color. I live by the motto that "it is better to be lucky than good, at least when it comes to dye lots."

Luster, Sheen, Colors, and Texture

The luster and sheen of a yarn can greatly affect how well texture shows up in a project. Multicolored, muted, or fuzzy yarns obscure all but the coarsest of textures. In other words, you just can't see the individual stitches, which is the essence of texture. Smooth, shiny yarns that reflect light are able to display intricate and delicate textures to their best advantage. However, this isn't necessary for lacy structures. In fact, a lacy structure should be considered a coarse structure because it can accommodate a wide variety of colors and luster in the yarn or thread, unless the yarn has a variable strand thickness or a very fuzzy texture, in which case the lacy structure can become obscured.

Drape Help for Knitters Trying Crochet

Drape is the ability of a fabric to flow. Crochet makes beautiful, intricate, and flowing fabrics but the yarn must be finer and softer than that used for knitting. For example, if you're making a sweater in which you would use a good, substantial, worsted-weight yarn for a knitted stockinette-stitch pattern, you would choose a softer and possibly (but not necessarily) lighter-weight yarn for a crocheted version. Trying to make the right yarn choices is the biggest reason that knitters become discouraged when starting in crochet, and it's the easiest problem to fix. (See "Lesson on Drape" at right for more information.)

Why is there such a difference between crochet and knitting? Knitting is really the tying of half a knot on a row and then tying another half knot on the next row. Crochet is the tying of a full knot on one row. By its very nature, crochet will make a stiffer fabric than knitting if you use the same yarn and similar-texture stitches for both crafts. Hence, there is a difference in the types and styles of yarns used for crochet and knitting. Crochet can make very delicate and intricate fabrics with great drape just as with knitting, but the yarn or thread must be chosen correctly. One way to avoid wasting your time is to make a swatch of the pattern with one ball of yarn. Observe the results and ask yourself a few questions. Do you like it? Is it what you were looking for? How does it move?

A fabric with good drape will easily bend and move when you pick it up. The same is true of yarn. There are good, stiff yarns perfect for knitting and beautifully soft yarns perfect for crochet. With practice, you'll begin to recognize yarn drape by look and feel. The following lesson explores this topic and sets up a basis for comparing yarns now and in the future.

Lesson on Drape

This lesson explores the drape of yarn. You'll learn to visualize the finished project in your head just by feeling the yarn.

1. Visit a yarn shop or any place with a wide variety of yarns, such as craft stores. (Note that a yarn shop will usually have employees with more yarn experience and can help you find what you're looking for.) Now go to the displays of yarn. Skip the novelty yarns for this lesson; they're difficult to determine drape with. Feel the yarns with your fingertips. Find a sport-weight or double knitting yarn, a soft worsted-weight yarn, and a firm worsted-weight yarn. Warning: If you're at a yarn shop and the store personnel are knitters, they will describe the firm worsted-weight yarn as a good, strong yarn. The yarn is exactly what a knitter needs but for the crocheter it will make a stiff, inflexible garment.

2. Purchase one skein each of a soft yarn and a firm yarn. Using a single crochet stitch, make an 8" x 8" swatch of each yarn. Pick up and feel each swatch, and *really* look at the results. Wave each swatch with your hands and look at how they move. Now take a strand of each yarn used. Look at it closely and feel it in your fingers. The differences in these yarns, both as a fabric and as single strands, are the essence of drape. Use this knowledge in the future for choosing yarns and repeat this lesson often with each new type of yarn you come across. This is one of the secrets of all those master crocheters and knitters you know. They have already repeated this exercise many, many times. Now that you know it, you can be a master too.

Crochet Hooks

The following sections describe the structure of crochet hooks, the variety of materials they are made from, and their sizes.

Hook Structure

A crochet hook consists of a hook, a throat, and a shaft.

Hook. The hook is at the tip, is curved to form a U shape, and catches the yarn.

Throat. The throat is adjacent to the hook. One style of crochet hook has a more rounded throat area, while the other style has a flattened throat area.

Shaft. The shaft, or handle, can be round, with a flattened area for your thumb and index finger, or can be shaped as an ellipse with an area for the thumb and index finger. The shaft can also be long or short. So which is the best one? It really depends on you and what you're doing. I have several different styles of hooks. I find that I like to change from project to project and yarn to yarn, and even from stitch to stitch. If you're a beginner, pay special attention to the section "Combinations of materials" on page 65 before deciding on a type of crochet hook to try first.

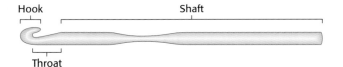

Types of Crochet Hooks

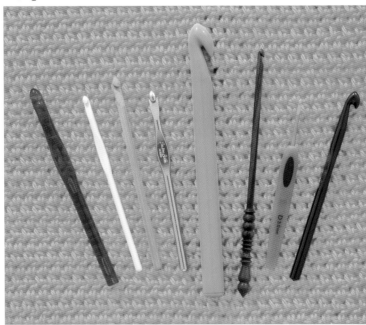

Aluminum. Aluminum crochet hooks are lightweight and work well for wool, wool blends, acrylic, acrylic blends, alpaca, and cotton. These are the hooks I use most often. There is just something I like about the feel of brushed metal in my hand. However, if you're sitting in a location that is cold, these hooks will quickly make your hands cold as well. This is due to the thermal conductivity of the metal.

Steel. These are very small hooks and are used for fine thread work. If you're using one of these, try a foam cover to ease the stress on your fingers.

Plastic. These hooks are lighter weight than aluminum crochet hooks, so they work well for the very large hooks in sizes L-11 (7.0 mm) and up. I also have a set of these in smaller sizes for plane rides. I have found that it can be a hassle to get through airport security with metal hooks, so I pack the metal hooks in my checked suitcases and take the plastic ones in my carry-on. I have to crochet when I fly because I'm not the world's greatest flyer. Every bump requires that I be able to think "sc in next st, hdc in next st, ch 1, turn."

Wood or bamboo. I prefer these hooks for working with slippery yarns like silk, silk blends, nylon, and nylon blends because they slow the yarn down across the shaft of the crochet hook. When I use metal or plastic hooks with slippery yarns, it feels as though I am slipping and sliding across ice. I need the extra bit of drag on the shaft to feel in control with these types of yarns.

Combinations of materials. There have been some wonderful advances in crochet hook design in recent years. I used the round-shaft-with-flattened-grip crochet hooks almost exclusively until I recently found Clover Soft Touch Crochet Hooks. These crochet hooks have an aluminum hook and throat, and part of the shaft is aluminum. The remainder of the shaft is made of molded rubber and plastic with an elliptical-shaped grip for easy use. I strongly urge all beginning crocheters to consider purchasing a couple of these crochet hooks. They will decrease your learning time because they require you to hold the hook correctly. I also encourage intermediate and experienced crocheters to try these hooks. You'll find them very comfortable, especially for hook sizes F-6 (4.0 mm) and below. I warn you though—you won't want to go back and you'll probably end up purchasing all the available sizes! Oh well! What's another couple of crochet hooks among friends anyway?

Ergonomic Crochet Hooks

For my fellow crocheters who are suffering from some form of arthritis or carpal tunnel syndrome, you may want to try the Clover Soft Touch Crochet Hook. You'll be able to hold the hook with a looser grip than any of the rounded-style hooks. You may also be able to crochet without pain. If you have been using the pencil grip for crocheting, consider changing to an overhand or knife grip (see "Holding the Crochet Hook" on page 68). This change in grip will decrease the pressure on your fingers, which should ease your symptoms.

Hook Sizes

If you're new to crochet, I need to help you out with hook sizes. First, regardless of how easy the alphabetic (G, H, I, J) or numeric (7, 8, 9, 10) size designations are, always look for the millimeter (mm) measurement.

Crochet hooks can be different measurement sizes but still have the same alphabetic or numeric designation. For instance, a size F-6 hook from several years ago was 3.75 mm, but the current size F-6 hooks are 4.0 mm. Yes, 0.25 mm will make a difference in your gauge and in the sizing of your projects. In addition, the Craft Yarn Council of America lists a 9.0 mm hook as size M-13, while some manufacturers label this hook N-13, as shown in the table below. Further, this is just among U.S. crochet hook sizes. If you have a pattern from the United Kingdom or Canada, the size is different depending on when the pattern was written, and is different from the U.S. size. These problems are eliminated when you use the metric measurement of the crochet hook. If you have an old set of crochet hooks and are not sure about the actual size, measure the shaft with a crochet hook sizing guide or a tape measure.

Crochet Hook Conversion Sizes

Metric Hook Sizes	U.S. Hook Sizes	U.K. Hook Sizes
2.25 mm	B-1	13
2.5 mm	C-2	12
3.0 mm		11
3.25 mm	D-3	10
3.5 mm	E-4	9
4.0 mm	F-6	8
4.5 mm	G-7	7
5.0 mm	H-8	6
5.5 mm	I-9	5
6.0 mm	J-10	4
6.5 mm	K-10½	3
7.0 mm	L-11	2
8.0 mm	M-12	1
9.0 mm	N-13	0
11.5 mm	P-15	
15.0 mm	Q	

The millimeter size is the most accurate for sizing hooks; the letter or number on the U.S. sizes may vary from manufacturer to manufacturer.

The Tools of Sweater Creation

What do you need to start crocheting sweaters? Many people will tell you that a crochet hook and a ball of yarn will do it. Well, not really. A ball of yarn and a crochet hook are what an intermediate or experienced crocheter needs to start on another project. A new crocheter will need a few more tools to get started. In addition to listing the tools you'll need, I have included answers to the "Why?" question for each of these items.

Yarn. Acrylic or wool-and-acrylic mix yarns are excellent choices for sweaters. Why? These yarns are easily found in craft stores, yarn shops, and department stores. They have good drape, are easy to use, and are relatively inexpensive.

Crochet hooks. You should have a whole set of hooks, including sizes F-6 to K-10.5 (4.0 mm to 6.5 mm), or at least sizes H-8, J-10, and N-13 (5.0, 6.0, and 9.0 mm). Why? You'll eventually buy a whole set anyway, so why not now? If budgets are tight, then the three sizes mentioned above will work well. They are a good mix of small but not too small, medium, and large but not gigantic hook sizes.

Basic how-to guide to crochet. Why? Without a manual, you'll just be frustrated.

Pattern. Why? You need a goal. Everyone needs a goal.

A tape measure and a 6" ruler. Why? The tape measure is to check the size of the garment. You need the ruler to determine your gauge, which is an absolute necessity when making a sweater. So, if you have been making afghans exclusively, where size doesn't matter as much as it does for garments, don't assume you can skip this step.

Yarn pins. Why? You'll need these to start setting your gauge.

Stitch counter. Why? You'll find these useful for making sleeves. Personally, I find them indispensable. I can't keep my place in any pattern over five steps!

A small pair of scissors or a thread cutter. Why? You'll need to cut your yarn. If you have small children, consider getting the thread cutter because it is safer if small fingers get a hold of it. Also, if you get the thread cutters that look like pendants, you can usually take them on airplanes because they just look like a necklace.

One wonderful bag, large enough for everything. Why only one bag? It keeps things all in one place and prevents clutter in the house. You'll find that your family, be that husband, children, cats, or dogs, will need time to adjust to a crocheter's special quirks. So let them adjust slowly before you have 20 bags full of stuff and three bookcases devoted to yarn. It is best to stay under the radar as long as possible in the beginning. Why a *wonderful* bag? Well, everything a crocheter has or does is wonderful.

Time to yourself. Why? You need to concentrate and everyone deserves some time for themselves. If it helps, I give you permission to take time for yourself to crochet each day. You may tell the kids, husband, friend, dog, or cat that I gave you permission. That way they can resent me rather than you. I can take it. I don't live with them!

Special Tips and Techniques

This section covers a series of instructions to help the beginning crocheter learn new techniques for holding yarn and achieving different yarn tensions with a variety of hand positions, as well as two ways to hold a crochet hook.

Holding the Yarn

If you're right-handed, you'll more than likely crochet with the hook in your right hand and the yarn in your left. If you're left-handed, everything is reversed. Let's start with threading the yarn through your fingers. There are three ways to thread your yarn.

Tight tension position (four-finger tension). This tensioning technique is the most secure and will give you the tightest tension on your stitches when used with a single strand of yarn. It is good for use with nylon cord, and crochet thread used for doilies. It is also appropriate when making weather-resistant outdoor clothing because you can obtain a tight weave for water resistance. This four-finger tension is also used for two- and three-yarn crocheting. Thread the yarn clockwise over the pinky finger and then weave the yarn back and forth through the rest of the fingers.

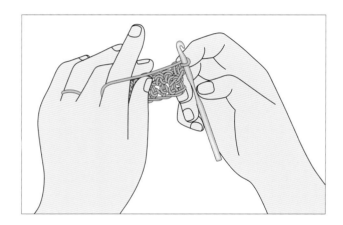

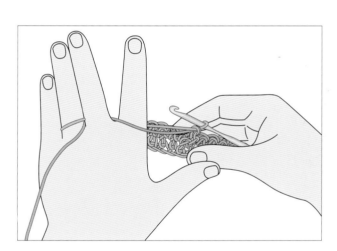

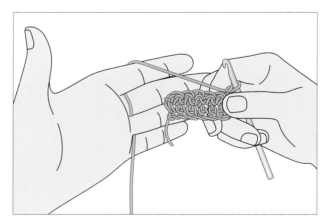

4-finger tension

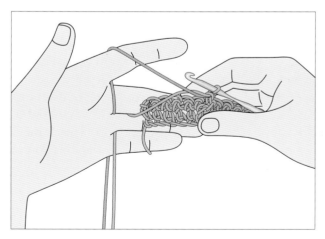

4-finger tension with
the 2-yarn variation

Medium tension position (three-finger tension). This is the most used tension for all types of crocheting and for most types of yarn. Thread the yarn clockwise between the ring and middle finger and then weave around middle finger and index finger.

Relaxed tension position (one-finger tension). This is the most relaxed position for yarn tension. It is used for thick and chunky yarns, as well as most of the novelty yarns. Thread yarn counterclockwise around your index finger.

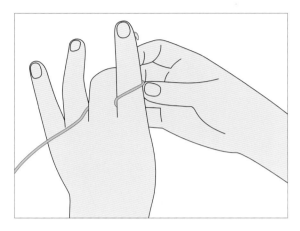

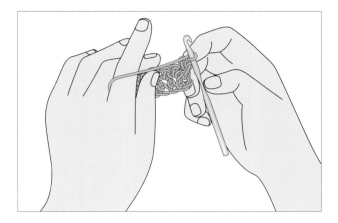

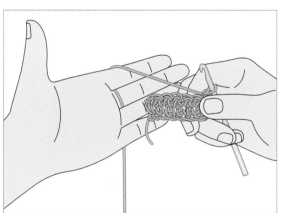

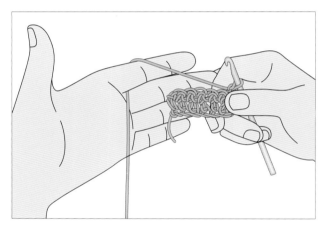

Holding the Crochet Hook

There are two ways to hold a crochet hook—overhand, or knife, grasp and pencil grasp.

Method 1: overhand grasp. The index finger and thumb are placed on each side of the flattened portion of the crochet hook. You'll find less movement of the hands is necessary when crocheting with this method than the next. The eased strain on your fingers with this hook position may help to ease your arthritis or carpal tunnel pain when crocheting.

Method 2: pencil grasp. The index finger and thumb are placed on each side of the flattened portion of the crochet hook. The shaft is allowed to rest in the crook of your hand.

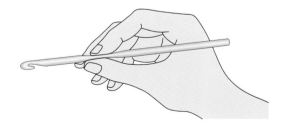

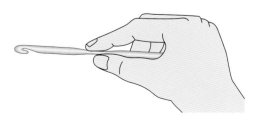

Index of Stitches

This section lists the stitches used in this book and provides step-by-step instructions and illustrations to help you learn how to make each stitch. Each project includes a list of stitches used, so you can look them up when you need them.

Slipknot

1. Form a loop with the yarn. Hold the loop with your fingers at the neck of the loop.
2. Insert the hook into the loop. Yarn over and bring the yarn through the loop.
3. Pull on both ends of the loop ends to gently tighten the slipknot on the hook.

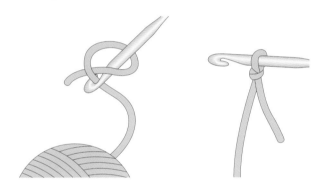

TIP: I must confess that I used to painstakingly tie a knot, like tying your shoelaces, onto the crochet hook instead of forming a slipknot. Frustrating, clumsy, and cumbersome are all good, descriptive adjectives for what I did. I don't understand how I missed the technique of starting with a slipknot, but a knitter corrected me. Have you ever had a moment when something dawns on you? It really is like a light turning on in your brain. Well, that was one of those times for me. Needless to say, I have never looked back.

Yarn Over (YO)

Make a yarn over by wrapping the yarn over the top of the hook in a clockwise direction.

Chain Stitch (ch)

Do not count the loop on the hook. It is a loop, not a chain.

1. Yarn over the hook and pull through the loop on the hook.
2. Repeat for the number of chains required.

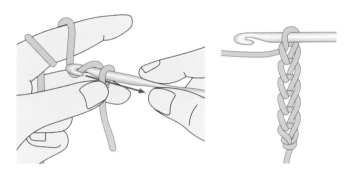

TIP: The second row of crochet can be difficult to make if the foundation chain stitches are too tight. This is easily solved by using a hook size one or two times larger than that specified in the pattern. After forming the foundation chain, switch back to the hook size specified in the pattern.

Slip Stitch (sl st)

1. Insert the hook in the stitch from the front to the back.
2. Yarn over (clockwise), bring up the loop, and then pull the loop through the loop on the hook.

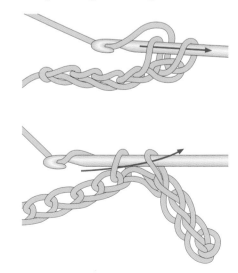

Overstitching

1. Holding the yarn above the piece, insert the hook into the piece around the stitch from front to back, and to the front again on the other side of the stitch.
2. Yarn over (clockwise), bring up the loop, and then pull the loop through the loop on the hook.

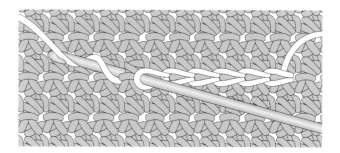

Applied Slip Stitch Crochet

1. Holding the hook above the piece and the yarn under the piece, insert the hook through the fabric, yarn over, and bring up a loop.
2. Insert the hook again in the next stitch or a little further, yarn over, bring up a loop, and then pull the loop through the loop on the hook.

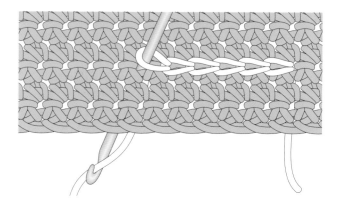

Single Crochet (sc)

1. Insert the hook in the stitch from the front to the back of the piece.
2. Yarn over and pull up the loop.
3. Yarn over and pull through both loops on the hook.

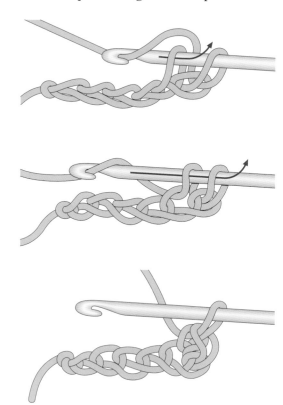

Back Single Crochet (bsc)

This stitch is worked like a single crochet except the hook inserts into the stitch from the back of the piece, whereas a single crochet inserts into the stitch from the front of the piece. *(Be careful with this stitch. Don't work in the front or back loop and don't go around a front or back post. Enter the main part of the stitch from the back to the front as shown in the illustration on page 71.)*

1. Insert the hook in the stitch from the back to the front of the piece.
2. Yarn over and pull up the loop.
3. Yarn over and pull through both loops on the hook as for regular single crochet.

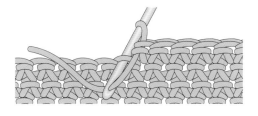

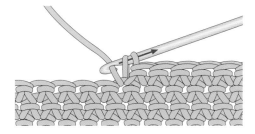

Reverse Single Crochet (rsc)

This stitch is used as an edging. Unlike other crochet stitches, this stitch is worked from left to right.

1. When finished with a piece, do not turn. Insert the hook into the stitch *before* the end stitch.
2. Yarn over, pull up the loop, yarn over, and pull through both loops on the hook.
3. Continue in this manner, inserting the hook into the next stitch to the right for each stitch.

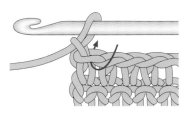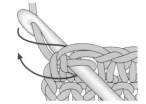

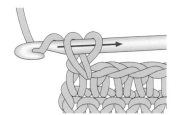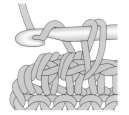

Half Double Crochet (hdc)

1. Yarn over, insert the hook in the stitch, yarn over, and pull up the loop (three loops on the hook).
2. Yarn over and pull through all three loops on the hook.

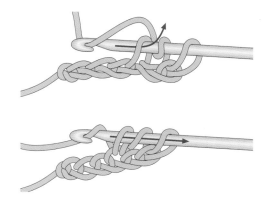

Double Crochet (dc)

1. Yarn over, insert the hook into the stitch, yarn over, and pull up the loop.
2. Yarn over and pull through only two loops on the hook.
3. Yarn over and pull through the remaining two loops on the hook.

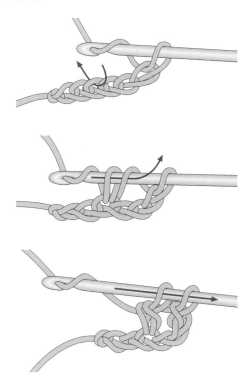

Ivy Stitch (Three-Spike Cluster)

This stitch is worked above a section with at least four rows of single crochet.

1. Insert hook in the stitch, one row down and two stitches back from the current position.
2. Yarn over and pull the loop up, yarn over, and pull the loop through one loop on the hook (two loops are on the hook).
3. Insert the hook in the hole, four rows down and one stitch forward, yarn over, and pull up the loop.
4. Yarn over and pull through one loop on the hook (three loops are remaining on the hook).
5. Insert the hook in the hole, one row down and three stitches forward, yarn over, and pull up the loop.
6. Yarn over and pull through the first loop on the hook (four loops are remaining on the hook).
7. Yarn over and pull through all four loops on the hook, and chain one. This makes an ivy stitch.

Beginning Star Stitch

This is the first stitch in a row of star stitches.

1. Chain four. Insert the hook in the second chain from the hook and pull up the loop.
2. (Insert the hook in the next chain and pull up the loop) twice.
3. (Insert the hook in the next stitch and pull up the loop) twice in the same stitch.
4. Yarn over and draw through all six loops on the hook, and chain one to close the star.

Star Stitch

1. Chain one, insert the hook in the eyelet of the beginning or previous star stitch, and pull up the loop.
2. Insert the hook through the last two loops on the left side of the previous star stitch and pull up the loop.
3. Insert the hook in the same stitch as the last stitch of the previous star stitch and pull up the loop.
4. (Insert the hook in the next stitch and pull up the loop) twice.

5. Yarn over and draw through all six loops on the hook.
6. Chain one to close the star stitch.

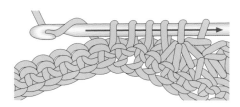

Popcorn Stitch

1. Work four double crochets into the same stitch.
2. Remove the hook from the loop.
3. Insert the hook through the top two loops of the first double crochet in the four-double-crochet group.
4. Reinsert the hook in the loop. Yarn over and draw through all the loops on the hook.

Modified Popcorn Stitch (m-pc)

This is worked after a row of double crochets.

1. Work three double crochets around the post of the double crochet of the previous row.
2. Remove the hook from the loop.
3. Insert the hook through the top two loops of the first double crochet in the three-double-crochet group.
4. Reinsert the hook in the loop. Yarn over and draw through all loops on the hook.

Beginning Cluster Stitch (Beg-CL)

This is the first stitch in a row of cluster stitches.

1. Yarn over, insert the hook into the stitch, yarn over, pull up a loop, yarn over, and pull through the first two loops on the hook.
2. (Yarn over, insert the hook in the same stitch, yarn over, pull up a loop, yarn over, and pull through the first two loops on the hook) twice.
3. Yarn over, pull up a loop through all four loops on the hook, and chain one. This completes the beginning cluster stitch.

Six-Cluster Stitch (6-CL)

1. Yarn over, insert the hook in the stitch, yarn over, bring up a loop, yarn over, and pull through two loops on the hook.
2. (Yarn over, insert in the same stitch, yarn over, bring up a loop, yarn over, and pull through first two loops on the hook) four times.
3. Yarn over, pull through all six loops on the hook, and chain one.

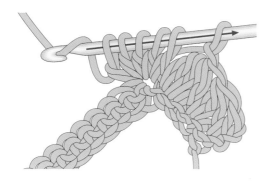

Seven-Cluster Stitch (7-CL)

1. Yarn over, insert the hook in the stitch, yarn over, bring up the loop, yarn over, and pull through two loops on the hook.
2. (Yarn over, insert in the same stitch, yarn over, bring up the loop, yarn over, and pull through two loops on the hook) five times until there are seven loops on the hook.
3. Yarn over, pull through all seven loops on the hook, and chain one.

Large Puff Stitch

1. (Yarn over, insert the hook in the stitch, yarn over, and pull up the loop); rep seven times in the same stitch.
2. Yarn over and pull through all 15 loops on the hook. Chain one. This makes a large puff stitch.

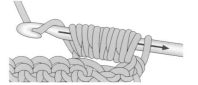

Small Puff Stitch

1. (Yarn over, insert the hook in the stitch, yarn over, and pull up the loop) four times in the same stitch.
2. Yarn over and pull through all nine loops on the hook. Chain one. This makes a small puff stitch.

Front-Stitch Double Crochet (FSdc)

This is *not* front-post double crochet (FPdc). Always work a regular double crochet for the first and last stitch of the row.

Yarn over, insert the hook from the front to the back into the stitch at the base of the current double crochet, then through to the next double crochet from the back to the front (see illustration). Complete the stitch as a normal double crochet.

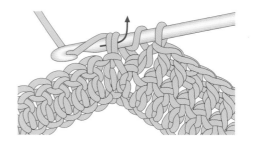

Back-Stitch Double Crochet (BSdc)

This is *not* back-post double crochet (BPdc). Always work a regular double crochet for the first and last stitch of the row.

Yarn over, insert the hook from the back to the front into the stitch at the base of the current double crochet, then through to the next double crochet from the front to the back (see illustration). Complete the stitch as a normal double crochet.

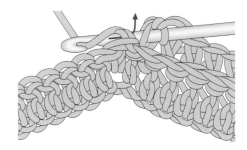

Increasing (inc)

Work two stitches into the same stitch. This increases by one stitch.

Decreasing (dec)

Work two stitches together. This decreases by one stitch.

Single crochet two stitches together (sc2tog): Insert the hook in the first stitch, yarn over, bring up the loop, insert the hook in the second stitch, yarn over, bring up the loop, yarn over, and bring through all three loops on the hook. Two single crochet stitches are crocheted together.

Double crochet two stitches together (dc2tog): Yarn over, insert the hook in the first stitch, yarn over, bring up the loop, yarn over, pull through two loops. Yarn over, insert the hook into the second stitch, yarn over, bring up the loop, yarn over, pull through two loops. Yarn over, pull through the remaining three loops on the hook. Two double crochet stitches are crocheted together.

Half double crochet two stitches together (hdc2tog): Yarn over, insert the hook in the first stitch, yarn over, pull up the loop. Yarn over, insert the hook in the second stitch, yarn over, pull up the loop. Yarn over, pull through all five loops on the hook. Two half double crochet stitches are crocheted together.

If you need to decrease in any other stitches, use this general formula to decrease: Bring up the first loop in one stitch and the next loop(s) in a second stitch. Continue with forming the rest of the stitch normally.

Weave Stitch Joining with a Slip Stitch

Place pieces side by side with wrong side facing up.

1. Attach the yarn at the bottom of the seam with a slip stitch.
2. Insert the hook into the edge stitch on the left-hand piece from front to back and make a slip stitch.
3. Insert the hook into the edge stitch on the right-hand piece from front to back and make a slip stitch.
4. Continue weaving back and forth over the seam as shown.

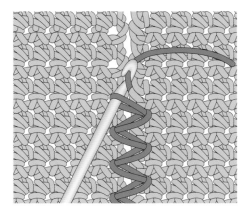

Weave Stitch Joining with a Needle

With the wrong side facing up and the seams together, weave the needle and yarn through the edges of the seams as shown.

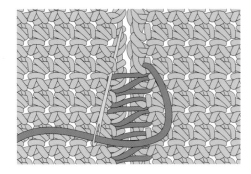

Gauge

Time is a funny thing. I never have time to make a gauge swatch, but I *always* have time to remake the sweater. I've learned from experience that making a gauge swatch is very important and shouldn't be overlooked. A gauge swatch helps determine the number of stitches you make per inch, which you use to predict the measurements of your project. In the following sections, you will practice working with loose and tight tensions in gauge swatches and discover how to measure your gauge.

Tension and Gauge Lesson

The most basic way to adjust your gauge is by changing your hook size. If your gauge swatch comes out with too many stitches per inch and is too small according to the pattern, go up a hook size and try again. If your gauge swatch comes out with too few stitches per inch and is too large, go down a hook size.

However, changing hook sizes does not correct all deviations in the tension of your stitches, which also affects your gauge. Generally, when you're tired, you'll find that your tension becomes too loose, and when you're under a lot of stress, your tension becomes too tight. Your garment will come out with the best results if your tension is even throughout.

Stitch tension is best corrected by feel rather than by sight. Your sight keeps your hook in the right place at the right time, so it's hard to concentrate on looking at the stitch tension at the same time. Experienced crocheters only *look* at stitch tension occasionally. They keep the tension the same, stitch to stitch, by feeling the tension. They may not even know they are doing it. I didn't realize it for a long time until a beginner asked me how I kept my stitches so even. The following tension and gauge lesson will help you develop this skill.

For practice, use a smooth yarn that specifies a size J-10 (6.0 mm) hook. Don't try this with a fuzzy, furry, or ribbon yarn because those will make it more difficult to crochet the swatch and to see the stitches. After you make a couple of easy projects, you'll be ready to try working with novelty yarn.

Exercise 1: To begin, chain 21. Single crochet in the second chain from the hook, single crochet in each chain across, chain one, and turn.

Now the lesson begins. Be sure to feel the yarn in your left (right) hand. Single crochet into the first stitch very, very loosely, single crochet in the next stitch and in each stitch across loosely, chain one, and turn. Do you notice how the yarn feels like it is tickling your fingers?

Single crochet in the first stitch and in each stitch across. Again, it is learning the feeling of creating a very loose gauge that is important, not the stitches. Repeat this step for a total of 10 rows.

Exercise 2: Repeat exercise 1, working with back single crochet stitch (bsc). This will give you a feeling for a forward stitch that enters the piece from the back to the front.

You have just learned to recognize when your tension is too loose for a stitch going forward and from front to back.

Exercises 3 and 4: Repeat exercises 1 and 2 with a tension that is too tight. Be sure to feel the yarn almost cutting through your fingers. Remember that it is the recognition of this feeling that is the purpose of these exercises.

Compare the sizes of the swatches you just made. See how changing your stitch tension affects your gauge? When working on a project, you'll find very quickly that just thinking of this lesson will cause you to automatically adjust your tension as needed.

Measuring Gauge Swatches

Each set of project instructions includes a section on gauge, providing you with the number of pattern stitches and rows in a 4" gauge swatch, and the hook size and yarn used to make the swatch. The following section gives you some practice with gauge, walking you through making gauge swatches for single crochet and back single crochet, and using these swatches to learn how to measure stitches and rows.

To begin, follow the directions below to make two swatches—single crochet and back single crochet. Then refer to the measuring instructions to fill in the blanks.

Single Crochet Gauge Swatch

Row 1: Ch 11 stitches. Single crochet in the second chain from the hook and in each remaining stitch across, chain one, and turn.

Row 2: Single crochet in first stitch and in each stitch across, chain one, and turn.

Repeat row 2 four more times. Tie off.

Number of rows_____ = 4"

Number of stitches_____ = 4"

Back Single Crochet Gauge Swatch

Row 1: Ch 11 stitches. Single crochet in the second chain from the hook and in each remaining stitch across, chain one, and turn.

Row 2: Back single crochet in first stitch and in each stitch across, chain one, and turn.

Repeat row 2 four more times.

Number of rows_____ = 4"

Number of stitches_____ = 4"

Once you make your swatches, compare their sizes. Are they the same? In a perfect world, they would be. Mine aren't. This illustrates the importance of always making a swatch of the stitch used in your pattern; even a stitch that enters on a different side of the fabric can give you a different gauge.

Now take your ruler and place it on the single crochet swatch so that the stitches line up along the ruler.

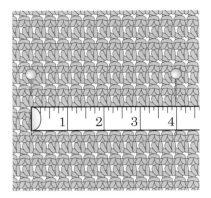

Measuring stitches

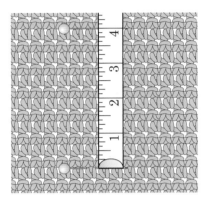

Measuring rows

With yarn pins, mark the position of the zero point of the ruler on the swatch and the 4" mark of the ruler on the swatch. Then change the ruler to measure the rows. Again, mark the position of the zero point and the 4" mark onto the swatch. Count the stitches within the yarn pins and the rows within the yarn pins and record the information in the spaces above left. Repeat this for the back single crochet swatch.

Now that you've practiced with these gauge swatches, you can use this same technique to measure the stitches and rows in your project gauge swatches. If you should find that your gauge does not match the gauge designated in the pattern, then you need to adjust your tension or your hook size until you obtain the proper gauge.

Caring for Sweaters

I am including this section because I have suffered tragedies trying to care for my sweaters that I would wish on no one else, and I want to share the lessons I've learned. One of my tragedies involved a beautiful alpaca-wool sweater which I decided to wash. Unfortunately, alpaca, hot water, and laundry detergent are incompatible! Can you imagine? One of my teddy bears now wears the lovely creation. After this incident, I began gathering information necessary to take better care of sweaters. I even found a process for "unshrinking" sweaters (see below). Although it works on superwash sheep's wool, acrylic, and cotton, don't expect this unshrinking technique to perform wonders with regular wool or alpaca—it failed me with those fibers.

Washing Sweaters

Sweaters should be hand washed, but I've also had good luck washing them in a machine. I turn them inside out to protect the buttons and wash them on the delicate cycle in lukewarm water, and then I allow them to dry in the air. *Never* dry sweaters in a dryer. I think it's important to make sure that children's apparel can withstand this type of washing treatment. Parents have enough things to do without having to hand wash their children's sweaters.

If you've crocheted a sweater out of alpaca or wool that is not superwash, do *not* let it agitate in the washing machine or it will felt and shrink so much that it will fit a doll. You can still machine wash these types of sweaters, but you must use special wool wash soap, such as Woolite, that does not require agitation or rinsing.

Unshrinking a Sweater

This procedure won't bring the article completely back to the original size but it will mitigate some of the effects and loosen up the stitches. You may at least be able to wear the sweater again but you may need to lose five pounds first. *Note that this process will not unshrink a sweater that has felted.*

1. Dissolve 1 ounce of borax in a couple tablespoons of hot water and add the mixture to a gallon of lukewarm water. Immerse the garment. Pull the garment gently to shape it. Rinse the garment in a solution of 1 gallon of warm water and 2 tablespoons of vinegar.

2. Dissolve 1 to 2 cups of noniodized salt in enough hot water to cover the garment. Let the garment stand in the solution for 2 hours. Then wash the garment in sudsy water. Rinse the garment three times in clean water. Then spin or roll the garment in towels.

3. Add ½ cup of detangling hair conditioner to a gallon of lukewarm water. Dip the garment until it is wet. Squeeze the garment but don't rinse. Shape the garment on a flat surface and let it dry.

Steaming and Blocking a Sweater

This procedure is the secret to keeping all hand crocheted and knitted items in the right shape.

Method 1: Place a very damp cloth on the sweater. Next, place a heated iron (use the heat setting appropriate for the yarn fibers in the garment, or the cotton setting if you're unsure) very close to the cloth, but do not let the iron touch the cloth. Continue until the sweater is evenly hot and humid. Stretch the sweater to the correct shape and allow it to dry.

Method 2: Use an iron on the steam setting to heat and humidify the sweater but don't let the iron touch the yarn. Continue until the sweater is evenly hot and humid. Stretch the sweater to the correct shape and allow it to dry.

Storing Sweaters

Store sweaters in a drawer or on a shelf. Never hang a sweater on a hook unless you're planning to use the sweater as part of your "Hunchback of Notre Dame" Halloween costume. If possible, place a cedar block in the drawer or on the closet shelf to ward off moths. Cedar smells much better than mothballs, and it's nontoxic. Every year, lightly sand the cedar block with sandpaper; this will release the scent that keeps the moths away.

Abbreviations

[]	Work instructions within brackets as many times as directed.
()	Work instructions within parentheses as many times as directed.
* *	Repeat instructions between asterisks as many times as directed or repeat from a given set of instructions.
alt	alternate
beg	begin(ning)
BSdc	back-stitch double crochet
BPdc	back-post double crochet
bsc	back single crochet
ch	chain or chain stitch
ch-	refers to chain or space previously made, such as ch-1 space
ch sp	chain space
CL	cluster
cont	continue(ing)
dc	double crochet
dc2tog	double crochet 2 stitches together
dec	decrease(ing)
FSdc	front-stitch double crochet
FPdc	front-post double crochet
g	gram(s)
hdc	half double crochet
hdc2tog	half double crochet 2 stitches together

inc	increase(ing)
lbs	pounds
lp(s)	loop(s)
m	meters
mos	months
m-pc	modified popcorn stitch
oz	ounces
patt	pattern
pkg	package
rem	remain(ing)
rep(s)	repeat(s)
RS	right side
rsc	reverse single crochet
sc	single crochet
sc2tog	single crochet 2 stitches together
sk	skip
sl st	slip stitch
sp(s)	space(s)
st(s)	stitch(es)
tch	turning ch
tog	together
WS	WS
yd(s)	yards
YO	yarn over

Resources

Bernat Inc.
www.bernat.com

Blumenthal Lansing Company
1929 Main Street
Lansing, IA 52151
Telephone: 563-538-4211
Fax: 563-538-4243
www.buttonsplus.com
Decorative Favorite Findings buttons: ivy leaves, cherries, ladybugs, flowers, lighthouse, sailboats, bird, fish, seashells
Decorative LaMode buttons: crayons, schoolbooks, pencils, dogs, schoolhouse, teddy bear, sunflowers, pansies, roses, chrysanthemums, daisies, irises, yellow butterfly, blue butterfly, bees with open wings, birdhouses
Decorative Streamline buttons: numbers, apples

Caron International Inc.
www.caron.com

Coats & Clark Inc.
www.coatsandclark.com

Herrschners
www.Herrschners.com
Red Heart Luster sheen—Gold

JHB International Inc.
1955 South Quince Street
Denver, CO 80231
Telephone: 1-303-751-8100
Fax: 1-303-752-0608
www.buttons.com
Decorative buttons: letters, silver clasp, beehives, smiling bees, bees with folded wings, brass bees, blue jays, cardinals, blue ducks

Lion Brand Yarn Company
www.LionBrand.com

New York Knits
1286 Blossom Drive
Victor, NY 14564
Telephone: 585-924-1950
Fax: 585-924-8909
www.newyorkknits.com
Sirdar yarn
Wendy yarn

Sirdar Inc.
www.sirdar.co.uk

Thomas B. Ramsden & Co, Ltd.
www.tbramsden.co.uk

The Village Yarn Shop
200 Midtown Plaza
Rochester, NY 14604
Telephone: 585-454-6064
Plymouth yarn

Yarn and Thread by Lisa
435 Boswell Suite #1
Crete, NE 68333
Telephone: 402-826-4278
Fax: 402-826-4288
www.yarn-and-threadbylisa.com

About the Author

Diane is originally from the great state of Montana, where most of her family still lives. She taught herself to crochet as a young child after her parents purchased a craft box at an auction. The box contained, among other things, yarn, crochet hooks, and a pattern book for making granny-square afghans. For the next 30 years, Diane concentrated on making baby blankets and afghans for friends, relatives, shut-ins, and anyone else who expressed an interest in one.

After the birth of her niece, Diane started making sweaters with encouragement from her group of knitting and crochet friends. After completing 10 sweaters, the idea of moving to the next step of designing sweaters seemed both daunting and exciting. Never one to shy from a challenge, Diane jumped right in with both feet.

Diane is currently working on the designs for her next crochet book. She lives in a 135-year-old house in upstate New York with "the girls." "The girls" are two mischievous Australian shepherds named Sarah and Lucy, whom Diane loves to distraction and spoils appropriately.